Q-870
16/498

D1801306

Powell's   Georgia Bellflowers (NoDJ)

16.00/4.98   NDJ

Antiques & Collectibles   105118

Georgia Bellflowers

THE FURNITURE OF
HENRY EUGENE THOMAS

Georgia Bellflowers

THE FURNITURE OF
HENRY EUGENE THOMAS

Ashley Callahan

Georgia Museum of Art
Athens, Georgia

January 14–April 15, 2012

©2011 Georgia Museum of Art, University of Georgia

Published by the Georgia Museum of Art, University of Georgia. All rights reserved. No part of this book may be reproduced without the written consent of the publishers.

Printed in China in an edition of 1,500 by Kings Time Printing Press, Ltd.

Design: MacFadden & Thorpe
Department of Publications: Hillary Brown and Mary Koon
Publications Interns: Katherine Jones and Nicollette Higgs

Library of Congress Cataloging-in-Publication Data

Callahan, Ashley.
  Georgia bellflowers : the furniture of Henry Eugene Thomas / Ashley Callahan.
       p. cm.
  Issued in connection with an exhibition held Jan. 14-Apr. 15, 2012, Georgia Museum of Art, Athens, Georgia.
  ISBN-13: 978-0-915977-77-2
  ISBN-10: 0-915977-77-X
  1. Thomas, Henry Eugene, 1883-1965--Exhibitions.
  2. Furniture--Georgia--History--20th century--Exhibitions. I. Thomas, Henry Eugene, 1883-1965. II. Georgia Museum of Art. III. Title.
       NK2439.T47A4 2011
       749.092--dc23

Partial support for the exhibitions and programs at the Georgia Museum of Art is provided by the W. Newton Morris Charitable Foundation and the Georgia Council for the Arts through the appropriations of the Georgia General Assembly. The Council is a partner agency of the National Endowment for the Arts. Individuals, foundations, and corporations provide additional support through their gifts to the University of Georgia Foundation.

This exhibition and publication are generously sponsored by Helen C. Griffith, the W. Newton Morris Charitable Foundation, and the Friends of the Georgia Museum of Art.

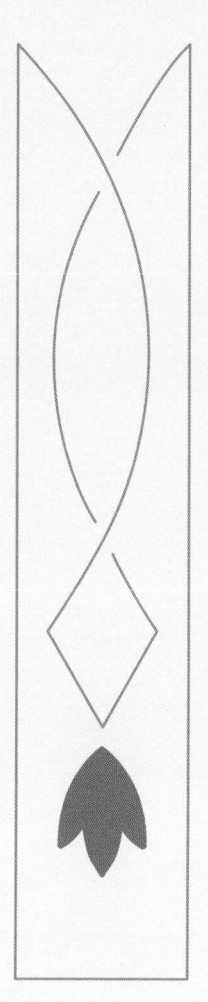

Thank You!

Lucy Allen
Nancy Allen
Heather James Anglin
Athens Historical Society
Stacey Thomas Beam
Upshaw Bentley
José Blanco
Connie Epps Bond
Ann Brackett
Mark Callahan
Diane Carter, Bank of America
Laura Carter
Center for Craft, Creativity and Design
Linda Chesnut
Janet Clark
John G. Collins
Morris H. Collins
Dale L. Couch
Paul Crater
Deanne Deavours
Burney S. Dobbs III
Carol Dolson
Gary L. Doster
William Underwood Eiland
David Epps
Nelle Price Epps
Jerry Epting
Katharine G. Farnham
Oscar P. Fitzgerald
Betty Alice Fowler
Peggy Galis
William R. Galt
Sally Gant
Betty Jane Gorham
Frances Gorham
Tom Granum
Frances Yates Green
Gwen Griffin
Fran Green Hilsman
Historic Boulevard Neighborhood Association
Mary Anne Hodgson
Laura Kittle Hunter
Julie Green Jenkins
Virginia and Arthur Kittle
Milton Leathers
Nan and Fred B. Leathers Sr.
Katie A. Lee
Barbara Lumpkin
Paul Manoguerra

Charlotte and George O. Marshall Jr.
Eve B. Mayes
Pete McCommons
Patsy B. McLeod
Stephen McLeod
Janet McPherson
Tricia Miller
Mr. and Mrs. Gilbert Milner
Annelies Mondi
Susan O'Brian
Josephine Paine
Glenn Paul
Berry Perkins
Adelaide and Graham Ponder
Betty Poss
Brenda and Jimmy Puckett
Bonnie Ramsey
Karen and Bucky Redwine
Robyn Reichling
Laura Doster Reid
Malcolm Richardson
Todd Rivers
Frank and Martha Puckett Roberts
Jeffie and Jack Rowland
Albert Sams Jr.
Sally Sams
Sharyn Sams
Nancy Scruggs
Christy Sinksen
J. David Smith
Marion Smith
Richard Smith
Jane Symmes
Ed Tant
Jill Kittle Thistle
Hazel H. Thomas
Robbie and John Thomas
Sara Thomas, Hardeman-Sams House
Margaret C. Totty
Lucy Tresp
Jim Trotochaud
Raúl Vázquez
Mary Bondurant Warren
John and Patty Whitehead
Ellen Wilkins Wiley
W. Thomas Wilfong
Peggy Sue Williams
Jennifer Wooten, Taylor-Grady House

This work was supported by a Craft Research Fund grant from
the University of North Carolina, Center for Craft, Creativity and Design.

Table of Contents

Acknowledgments
Annelies Mondi
8

Introduction
Dale L. Couch
11

Georgia Bellflowers:
The Furniture of Henry Eugene Thomas
Ashley Callahan
15

Endnotes
77

The Story of My Dad and
His Part in the Antiques Business
Jack Thomas
85

Checklist of the Exhibition
106

Acknowledgments

Though I moved to Athens many years after Henry Eugene "Gene" Thomas passed away, he has always been a part of the town for me. I have often heard of Gene Thomas and his wondrous skills as a wood worker and furniture picker. Once, shortly after graduating from the University of Georgia, I nearly rented a room in a house on Nacoochee Avenue in the Boulevard neighborhood; I later learned that this was the very same house with a backyard shop where Gene Thomas had lived and created so many beautiful pieces of furniture decades earlier. For the past twenty-five years I have resided in this same neighborhood. Many of my friends and neighbors own homes that Gene Thomas's family helped build or in which they lived, and I have met many people in the Athens community and beyond who are proud owners of his furniture.

My fondest connection to Gene Thomas, however, was my friendship with Henry Green, for whom the decorative arts program at the Georgia Museum of Art is named. Mr. Green loved telling me stories about his adventures with Gene as they canvassed the back roads of Georgia looking for old furnishings, and I loved hearing them. Mr. Green related how he had learned so much about styles of furniture, techniques of craftsmanship, and types of wood from Mr. Thomas. I am thankful that he freely shared with me his enthusiasm for Gene Thomas's skill and knowledge. Mr. Green's wife, Fran, and their family continue to ignite curiosity about Thomas's work, and it is because of their interest that the idea for this project came to light.

Ashley Callahan, the former curator of the Henry D. Green Center for the Study of the Decorative Arts at the Georgia Museum of Art, caught the spark and blew life into the project. She and I have been talking for years about how Gene Thomas is an important part of Athens history and about the need to document and promote his work. I am happy that she chose to take on the endeavor, one that furthers the museum's mission and creates a special opportunity to celebrate an artist dear to Mr. Green and important to the history of Georgia's decorative arts.

Because I have long marveled at the craftsmanship and elegance of Thomas's furniture, I am honored and proud to have served as in-house coordinator to help make this undertaking become a reality. For me, Gene Thomas is inextricably linked to Athens, and it was a pleasure to have the opportunity to meet members of his family. I am especially thankful to Hazel Thomas for allowing us to publish her husband Jack's lovely manuscript and to the entire family for their many contributions. I am also grateful to all of the people who graciously opened their homes to me, Ashley, and staff members of the museum. This undertaking greatly benefited from the effort and enthusiasm of Gene Thomas's family and the support of the community.

I greatly admire and appreciate Ashley's diligent research and perseverance in so many details related to Eugene Thomas's life and career. In this catalogue, thoughtfully designed by Brett MacFadden of MacFadden and Thorpe, and its accompanying exhibition, she astutely tells a cohesive and remarkable story about a skilled Athenian craftsman who has been long overlooked but whose talent is rare and significant.

Annelies Mondi
Deputy Director
Georgia Museum of Art

*GENE THOMAS, CA. 1940.
COLLECTION OF HAZEL H. THOMAS.*

Introduction

HENRY EUGENE THOMAS is of interest to historians of Georgia furniture for a number of reasons. First, he was a prominent figure in the first generation of collectors from Georgia and operated during the first recovery of furniture from Piedmont Georgia. Not only did Thomas discover many of the masterpieces that are now icons of early Georgia furniture, he also restored many of them. In these ways, Thomas was a bridge between Georgia material culture of the eighteenth and nineteenth centuries and the connoisseur-collectors of recent decades. He was an associate and friend of collector Henry D. Green and worked closely with the legendary Athens dealer Jake Bernstein. Perhaps most important, and most overlooked by scholars, is the fact that Thomas was a significant craftsman in his own right, who created a recognizable Colonial Revival style from the 1920s through the 1950s and provided furnishings for many prominent homes in Athens.

For Thomas, the collecting, restoring, and reproducing of fine examples of furniture found in the Piedmont was a seamless activity. The hard boundaries of period work and revival work likely seemed unified to him through the lens of style. Some modern collectors are suspicious of his name, fearing he might have made "improvements" to period finds. In fact, I first heard Thomas's name in 1980, in connection to a warning that his inlay was so good that collectors worried his work might be mistaken for period work. This suspicion itself acknowledges his talent and skill. In a different time and in acting upon a different ethos, it is likely that some clients requested improvements to their own pieces of furniture, both heirlooms and "finds." Considerable evidence of his character suggests that he would not have stylistically altered pieces to sell them as fakes, though that does not preclude later sellers from misrepresenting, unintentionally or not, his furniture. Yet the advanced collectors of the day, Henry Green included, would have been alert to such alteration. Whatever questions remain, the truth cannot hide from the eventual scientific connoisseurship that is bound to bear upon these works of Piedmont craft. And, thanks in part to this study, it is likely that Thomas will be remembered for his craft rather than the concern regarding authenticity that his work raised among collectors in the 1970s and 1980s.

Ironically, any furniture "improvements" originated from Thomas's own aesthetic, which he borrowed from the regional vernacular to create a new style of Piedmont Colonial Revival, the basis for requests that he alter or "improve" examples of period furniture. I know of no other regional style of Colonial Revival so specifically rooted in local examples. While much of the country persisted in a hybridized, multisourced Colonial Revival, Athens enjoyed a distinct style based in its regional Federal furniture. That alone is a remarkable accomplishment for Thomas.

Today we approach Thomas with a frank admiration for his own craft and for the style he fostered. His blend of historic Piedmont detail and modern form is best seen in a coffee table he made. Preposterous as an early example, it nonetheless conveys a fine aesthetic and provides admirable expression of a craftsman with a foot in two different times.

Of course, some of his work is period correct, such as his end tables, and he worked out of his scrap pile of early components as often as he sought new lumber. Yet his work is not fakery, and it is immediately recognizable for the time in which it was made and as having a distinctly local flavor.

With characteristic insight, Ashley Callahan presents an analysis of a man and his work that would have been lost to legend had she not acted. It is true that the generation who knew this artisan is fast fading. Callahan took the opportunity to retrieve and conserve the history of this important craftsman, and at the same time presents his work anew and independently to stand on its own merits. At the end of the day, Gene Thomas is not just a dealer/restorer. He is an artisan whose eye and work conditioned the taste of collector and noncollector alike, a man whose predilections helped forge a desire for Piedmont furniture that lives on today. He accommodated that demand not only with important discoveries of local antiques, but with a fine oeuvre of furniture that is meritorious in its own right.

Callahan has simultaneously traced the genealogy of collectors' preferences and uncovered a remnant of a "later" past. In doing so, she has advanced a view of the history of Georgia furniture that is not myopic and does not cease at the mere development of, say, the circular saw. From her perspective, the Georgia experience is as seamlessly connected to the past as it was for Thomas. Callahan demonstrates an oft-overlooked fact of life: we must understand recent history to understand remote history.

Dale L. Couch
Adjunct Curator, Henry D. Green Center for the Study of the Decorative Arts
Georgia Museum of Art

Fig. 1

Fig. 1
Arthur V. Clifton (1879–1956, active Athens, Georgia, ca. 1888–1913, then active Atlanta, Georgia). Portrait of Henry Eugene Thomas, ca. 1910. Photograph mounted on board. Board: 10 x 6 inches; Photograph: 5⅝ x 3⅞ inches. Collection of Frank and Martha Puckett Roberts.

Georgia Bellflowers: The Furniture of Henry Eugene Thomas

> "[Henry Eugene Thomas] was a most unusual man: a talented cabinetmaker who could make furniture by hand as authentically and skillfully as an eighteenth-century craftsman; a collector who would drop everything and take off without hesitation to look for antiques in houses, attics, barns, or anywhere else they were to be found. . . ."
>
> HENRY D. GREEN, 1976[1]

From the 1920s through the 1950s, Henry Eugene Thomas (fig. 1) worked from his home in Athens, Georgia, as an antiques dealer and furniture maker. He searched the area surrounding Athens for fine antiques that he sold to local collectors and regional and national dealers. He also made his own furniture in the style of the antiques he saw. Despite his success as a furniture maker, reflected in customer demand if not in any great fiscal recompense, by the turn of the twenty-first century his name was largely unknown. Several factors complicate documenting his life and career, including a lack of business records, the recent passing of family members with intimate knowledge of his work, and the loss of clear attributions as unlabeled furniture is bequeathed to younger generations. The willingness of his relatives and longtime Athenians to share their memories, however, and the documents related to particularly significant relationships—with his son, Jack Thomas, and with his friend Henry D. Green (1909–2003), one of the first advocates for the study of Georgia furniture—made this research possible. From these impressions and recollections emerge the story of a man devoted to antiques and passionate about woods, a skilled craftsman and a spirited individual. His work combines elements of historical styles and regional details, in particular a distinctive bellflower inlay design, with local woods and a range of construction techniques that primarily reflect traditional practices.

Gene Thomas found and created furniture against the backdrop of the Colonial Revival.² Architectural historian Richard Guy Wilson describes the Colonial Revival as an attitude, rather than a formal style or movement, that permeated all aspects of arts and culture in American life.³ It fluidly incorporates inspirations from the late seventeenth century to the mid-nineteenth century, often with multiple influences in anachronistic combinations, and is characterized by nostalgia for a "golden age" in America's past. One motivating factor behind the Colonial Revival's popularity was a reaction against modernism, a distaste Gene Thomas shared. One of his granddaughters, Laura Kittle Hunter, recalls, "I remember him talking about modern design and how he hated it. He absolutely hated it," and when his daughter Jo Anne, Laura's mother, redesigned one of the rooms in their house in a modern style, he clearly expressed his displeasure and made her change it back.⁴

The Colonial Revival started to thrive around the time of the Philadelphia Centennial Exposition in 1876 as Americans reflected on the history of their country and the objects and places associated with its founders. Collectors, especially in the northern United States, began scouring the countryside for antiques.⁵ Though much Colonial Revival furniture was (and is) mass produced, its style recalls a period when furniture was handmade, an association that gained moral cachet during the Arts and Crafts Movement.⁶ Also, the simplicity of much Colonial Revival furniture, at least when compared with the ornateness of Victorian furniture, appealed to homeowners in the early twentieth century learning about new ideas of domestic hygiene. The 1920s saw many milestones in the promotion of the Colonial Revival and the antiques that inspired it: the Metropolitan Museum of Art opened its American Wing in 1924, John D. Rockefeller Jr. began the restoration of Colonial Williamsburg in 1926 and the first of its traditional crafts shops opened in 1937, and Henry Ford established his Edison Institute (now the Henry Ford Museum and Greenfield Village) in 1929.

Although Gene Thomas did not advertise and did not formally describe his furniture as Colonial Revival, his customers would have been familiar with promotions for the style in the newspapers and magazines they read. They would have had ample opportunity to familiarize themselves with historic styles through the plethora of books, magazines, and auction catalogues published in the first decades of the twentieth century addressing and romanticizing American antiques. Wilson notes that one of the motivating factors in the popularity of the Colonial Revival is "ancestor worship" or "pride in genealogy," and advertisements repeatedly touted the American-ness of the style and promoted connections to George Washington and other founding fathers.[7] This emphasis on nationalism found an eager audience following the social upheaval caused by World War I and the influx of European immigrants into the United States. William B. Rhoads, in his essay on the Colonial Revival in American craft, quotes an advertisement from 1926 by the Danersk furniture company that praises American antiques, "These ancient symbols are dear to all true Americans. . . . We count it our duty to make them live again in convenient forms for the homes of our generation." The advertisement also lauds the new furniture's ability to better the lives of the people who use it: "the 'character and integrity' of the Founding Fathers 'will be fostered in our children if we surround them in their homes today with furniture that breathes the spirit of the best American traditions.'"[8] Gene Thomas's furniture offered his patrons a way to honor not just their national heritage, but their southern heritage as well.

In the first half of the twentieth century, ideas and attitudes surrounding the Colonial Revival found a receptive population in Athens, a town established in 1801 as the home of the University of Georgia. Athens was spared the ravages of General William T. Sherman's troops during the Civil War, so several streets still were (and are) lined with antebellum, white-columned mansions, and majestic new homes more often reflected the influence of those buildings than that of any more modern architectural style. Groups such as the United Daughters of the Confederacy (UDC) and the Daughters of the American Revolution (DAR) were active, as was the Garden Club of Georgia, which in 1946 dedicated a memorial to the founders of the Ladies Garden Club of Athens (the first organization of its type in the country, founded in 1891). The town experienced rapid growth and modernization during this period, more than doubling in population and increasing its citizens' access to such modern amenities as electricity and indoor plumbing.[9] Gene Thomas took advantage of some aspects of contemporary life in Athens, including riding the streetcar to town, and benefited from the interest in history evidenced and generated by groups such as the UDC and the DAR. Though it does not appear that he had any direct involvement with the University of Georgia, the school helped foster and finance a population interested in preserving the past.

During recent decades, Colonial Revival decorative arts have received increasing attention from collectors and museums.[10] The first works were collected for their high level of craftsmanship and for the faithfulness of their designs to the antiques they copied. Less attention has been paid to smaller shops outside of urban centers and to works produced later in the twentieth century. The relationship between the high-style urban furniture of the Colonial Revival and its rural counterparts mirrors that between the earlier urban and rural furniture it emulates, with rural cabinetmakers echoing urban designs, often with less sophistication but adding interesting regional interpretations. The scholarship addressing Colonial Revival works has progressed mostly from city to country and from earlier to later, placing Gene Thomas near the end of the queue. When evaluating Colonial Revival furniture and antiques "restored" during the period, it is important to acknowledge that the perception of authenticity has shifted in the intervening decades. Many changes made to antiques by craftsmen like Thomas might seem heavy-handed and unacceptable by current standards, but at the time these methods and actions generally were accepted as appropriate. Many craftsmen and their patrons simply wanted functional objects with an old-fashioned look.

Although modernists criticized the Colonial Revival for its "stifling of originality," Gene Thomas's furniture does exhibit creativity, especially in its deviations from design sources.[11] His unique approach to blending old and new and the difficulty of clearly categorizing his work and career make evaluating them more challenging and intriguing. A study of his career illustrates the role of the individual, nonurban craftsman in the Colonial Revival, and understanding his role as a dealer of antiques is important to the study of Georgia's late-eighteenth- and nineteenth-century decorative arts. The objects he created are notable examples of twentieth-century American craft, and he should be acknowledged as one of Georgia's finest craftsmen. Though many aspects of his biography have been lost over time, the following text presents much of the story of Gene Thomas's life and career.

Henry Eugene "Gene" Thomas was born February 7, 1883, in Lula, Georgia (Hall County), which is near Gainesville, in the northeastern part of the state, to Henry Nathaniel Thomas (1859–1922) and Henrietta DeLaPierre Buffington (fig. 2; 1862–1916). He was the oldest of his siblings: Martha Montine (Griffith, 1884–1951), Samuel Tillman (1887–1916), John Wilburn (1888–1935), Nellie (McElheney, 1889–1977), Eula Delceta (Collins, 1893–1950), Bertha Ann (Poss,

1894–1981), and Ruby Nanette (Parr, 1896–1971). The family moved to Athens when Gene was young, but they continued to spend time in Hall County and neighboring Jackson County.[12] According to the 1900 census, the Thomases lived in Athens on Nacoochee Avenue, in the Boulevard neighborhood—a new streetcar suburb (now a historic district) northwest of downtown Athens—where parts of the family continued to reside for several generations. Gene attended school in Athens; he had blue eyes and brown hair and went by the apt nickname "Shorty."

Nathaniel Thomas worked in many professions: as a farmer when the family lived in the country, a policeman when they moved to town, a house carpenter, and a distiller.[13] Gene and his two brothers helped their father build the homes at the northwest (where Nathaniel and Henrietta lived) and northeast corners of the intersection of Nacoochee and Boulevard, hauling the lumber on ox-drawn carts from Lula.[14] He served as a police captain for at least a decade and is shown in uniform in figure 3. Regarding Nathaniel's work as a distiller, his grandson Jack Thomas described him as "truly an artist at the still" and noted that "when whiskey making was legal he had a still going all the time."[15] Nathaniel ran two dispensaries, one operated by John A. Fowler off Prince Avenue and the other probably the Athens Dispensary on East Broad Street.[16] He may have passed this craft on to Gene, judging by the moonshine recipes the current owners of Gene's home found written on the walls of his shop.[17]

On December 18, 1907, Gene married Ethel Mae Epps (1889–1986), whom he called "Miss Annie," at her parents' home on Hancock Avenue, surrounded by family and friends and by decorations of bamboo, smilax, and holly (fig. 4).[18] Ethel came from a large family who had been in Athens for a long time.[19] Gene began building their "honeymoon house" at 835 Boulevard, near the intersection with Nacoochee, in 1906 and completed it in 1907.[20] When they married, he was a carpenter and, according to Ethel, he worked "for $1 a day—10 cents an hour, 10 hours a day."[21] One carpentry job that he completed before marrying was the transformation of a large Victorian home on Boulevard, known as the Morris house, into a Southern Colonial–style home with massive white columns in 1903.[22] In 1908, the couple spent several months in Dillard in the mountains of northeast Georgia, a trip they referred to as their honeymoon and during which Gene built a home (fig. 5) for Mrs. Asbury Hodgson, wife of a prominent Athens businessman.[23]

Gene and Ethel's first two children, Dorothy Lee "Dot" (Pendley, ca. 1910–1969) and Mildred Henrietta "Mit" (Martin, 1911–1949), were born in the house on Boulevard. The family then moved to the Smith house at the top of the Boulevard hill, where their next two children, Sarah (Gulledge, 1913–1947) and Samuel Jackson "Jack" (1915–1997), were born. Ethel's father gave her twenty-five acres of land on the old Epps Bridge Road (southwest of downtown Athens, along the Middle Oconee River), and they lived there for about two years, across from her brother Ben Epps (1888–1937), the renowned aviator.[24] In 1919, the Thomases moved to 245 Nacoochee Avenue, where their last two children, Ethlyn Eugenia "Jeannie" (Puckett, 1921–1953) and Jo Anne (Kittle, 1927–1982), were born and where Gene lived for the rest of his life (fig. 6). Jack described the move to town:

> On New Year's day, 1919, Ned Telfair, a black man who worked for my grandpa, came to our house on the Epps Bridge Road. He was driving Grandpa's two mules hitched to the wagon, and he and Dad started loading our furniture. We were moving to town.
>
> I . . . got on the wagon between Mama and Ned. My sisters were on the back of the wagon for the ride to town. Dad rode his bicycle in. . . .
>
> The first day we were there on Nacoochee, I could hardly wait for night to come so I could see those strange things hanging down in the middle of every room light up. . . . At dark Dad reached up to the cord in the kitchen and turned a button and the room was suddenly bright with light. It scared me at first but in about ten minutes I would go up to it and look at the little red-gold wire in it that made the light. Everybody in the family was thrilled to have lights that you didn't have to light with a match. . . .[25]

Jack described the Victorian home as having "a porch all across the front and around the side on the north," with "large turned posts with turned [balusters] between the posts."[26] Gene later altered the porch, replacing the posts and balusters with craftsman-style, square tapered columns on stone and concrete pillars, the top of one of which he inscribed "by H. E. Thomas/ July 7–1931" (figs. 7 and 8). At this home, which has a large backyard, they always had chickens, a garden, and sometimes pigs and a cow.[27] In the late 1910s, the family attended the

Fig. 2
Henrietta Buffington, original ca. 1890s reproduction of a painted photograph. Collection of Frank and Martha Puckett Roberts.

Fig. 3
Nathaniel Thomas, original ca. 1907 reproduction of a photograph. Collection of Hazel H. Thomas.

Fig. 4
Ethel Epps and Eugene Thomas wedding portrait, 1907. Photograph. 5½ x 3⅞ inches. Collection of Barbara Lumpkin.

Fig. 2

Fig. 3

Fig. 4

Fig. 5

Fig. 6

Fig. 7

Fig. 8

Fig. 5
Mountain home of Mrs. Asbury Hodgson, Dillard, Georgia, built by Gene Thomas in 1908. Hand-tinted photograph. Collection of Malcolm Richardson.

Fig. 6
Thomas family, ca. 1935 (l-r standing: Gene, Ethel, Dot, Mildred, Sarah, Jack; l-r seated: Jo Anne, Eugenia). Photograph. Collection of Hazel H. Thomas.

Fig. 7
Home of the Thomas family, 245 Nacoochee Avenue, Athens, Georgia, n.d. Photograph. Collection of Jill Kittle Thistle.

Fig. 8
Gene Thomas's signature on the pillar at his home on Nacoochee Avenue. Photograph by author.

Baptist Tabernacle on Childs Street (until it burned), then, later, the Prince Avenue Baptist Church, where Ethel was a charter member.[28] Later in life, Gene did not attend church, but his grandchildren remember him always having a Bible in hand when he was not in his shop.[29]

Gene and Ethel's son, Jack (fig. 9), worked as a plumber, an electrician, and an auctioneer. He married Hazel Haynes in 1937 and earned the title "Mayor of Boulevard" because of his efforts to promote and protect the history and character of the neighborhood.[30] He wrote columns for the *Athens Observer* from January 1974 to April 1976 and from July 1987 to March 1991 and for the *Banner-Herald* from May 1976 to June 1987. Although many of the columns address politics and current events, quite a few are stories about his family and the history of Athens. Some of these stories are invaluable as documents of his father's work with furniture; others provide colorful details about his daily life, including that Gene loved to "mix syrup and butter and then ladle it on to his biscuit with his knife" or that he decided to add a second seat to the family's outhouse in case someone was in a rush and the first was occupied.[31] Jack's columns and a previously unpublished manuscript he wrote in 1986 titled "The Story of My Dad and His Part in the Antiques Business," which appears in this volume, are key resources in the study of Gene's life and work.

Jack noted that after moving back to Nacoochee his father "was working regularly as a finishing carpenter."[32] He described his father's role in building a home: "When Dad did carpentry work, it was always his job to stay on after the usual run of the mill work and finish up the fine bookshelves, picture moldings, and the intricate dentil work that went into making a fine house a superb mansion."[33] One of his carpentry jobs was in 1922 for Mrs. B. F. Hardeman's home, now known as the Hardeman-Sams House, on Milledge Avenue, a main thoroughfare in Athens lined with many impressive mid-nineteenth-century white-columned structures.[34] He made four mantels, two of which remain in the house. Jack described the project: "She wanted the finest patterns available, with sunburst carvings in the middle and one on each side leg or standard. Dad set to work and carved the sunbursts by hand. He put the mantels together and then added the most beautiful moldings. Mrs. Hardeman was thrilled to no end with them when they were set."[35] According to Janet Clark, a tour guide at the Church-Waddel-Brumby House (built in 1820 and now the Athens Welcome Center), the mantels are copies of the ones there, which are based on a design by American architect Asher Benjamin (1773–1845).[36] Mrs. Hardeman sold the house in 1932 to Walter A. Sams, who gave "hand-carved Federal mantels," also described as copies of those at the Brumby House, to the Phi Mu sorority house across the street in the 1960s, possibly some of the originals that Gene carved for Mrs. Hardeman.[37]

Gene also worked on the James R. White Jr. House on Prince Avenue, at the corner of Nacoochee, designed by Atlanta architect Neel Reid (1885–1926) and completed ca. 1923 (fig. 10).[38] This house, which is just down the street from where Gene lived, later served as the home of the Kappa Delta sorority and now is home to the Delta Tau Delta fraternity. Jack especially enjoyed this project because Mr. White allowed him to read in his library while Gene finished the fine trim. Of particular note in this house is the freestanding curved staircase Gene constructed.[39] Gene's grandson John Thomas (Jack's son) recalls hearing about a staircase of his grandfather's, likely this one, that attracted much attention, explaining that, "for a while, carpenters were coming from all over the South to see it."[40] Another home for which Gene did the millwork was "Tip Top," a replica of Tara from the movie *Gone with the Wind* (1939), built by local physician Dr. Harry Erwin Talmadge (1907–1994) around 1940 several miles west of downtown Athens overlooking the Middle Oconee River in what is now the Forest Heights neighborhood (fig. 11).[41]

Gene Thomas certainly worked on many more homes in Athens than the few described here, but documenting additional projects is difficult as he did not keep formal (or informal) records and these are the only buildings that the individuals interviewed recall. What is notable about these samples of his work is that they include fine examples of the Colonial Revival style. Neel Reid is the foremost classicist of Georgia's architects of the early twentieth century, and his designs were and are revered as the epitome of refined taste and style. That Gene worked on such an impressive home for such a renowned architect, contributing and executing details certain to draw attention, demonstrates that his work was held in high regard. Helping recreate the fictional home of Scarlett O'Hara firmly places his work within the southern interpretation of the Colonial Revival style.

How Gene gained his carpentry skills is not documented, but he likely learned at least some of his trade from his father and possibly from his uncles. Nathaniel's brother Dilmus Oscar (1861–1925) listed his profession as house carpenter in the 1910 census, which records his address as 245 Boulevard. Gene's daughter Jo Anne and her family later owned that home, which members of the Thomas family may have built.[42] That

Fig. 9
Jack Thomas celebrating his fiftieth wedding anniversary, 1987. Collection of Hazel H. Thomas.

Fig. 10
The James R. White Jr. House, 1924. Photograph by Robert Flowers (active Atlanta, Georgia). Private collection.

Fig. 9

Fig. 10

Fig. 11

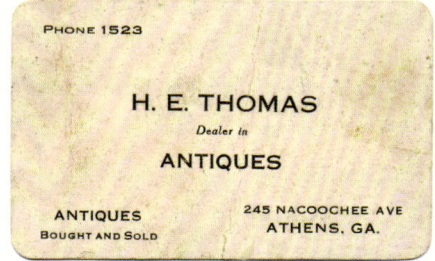

Fig. 12

Fig. 13

Fig. 11
Vintage postcard of the home of Dr. Harry E. Talmadge, Athens, Georgia, n.d. Published by the Asheville Post Card Company (Asheville, North Carolina). Private collection.

Fig. 12
Business card, n.d. 2³⁄₈ x 3⁷⁄₈ inches. Collection of Hazel H. Thomas.

Fig. 13
Vintage postcard of Noah's Ark, Abbeville, South Carolina, n.d. Private collection.

census also lists Gene's brother-in-law John Wesley McElheney (1880–1958), his sister Nellie's husband, as a house carpenter, living at 175 Nacoochee. The Thomases continued living in and visiting rural Georgia for many decades, and they may have had opportunities to learn some skills from furniture makers working in the Lula area.⁴³ Many individuals have described Gene Thomas as self-taught, but his high level of skill, specialization in finishing carpentry, and familiarity with old-time methods (according to Jack's descriptions), suggest that he or his family may have had at least some informal connection to earlier craftsmen.

In the 1910s and early 1920s, Gene's pastimes included hunting and fishing with his brothers, playing the violin, and attending baseball games at the University of Georgia with Jack.⁴⁴ While his grandchildren and others who knew him later in his life remember him as somewhat reserved—interested only in antiques and his Bible—Jack's writings suggest that his father was an entertaining storyteller earlier in his life. When Charles Salter profiled Jack in his popular Georgia Rambler column for the *Atlanta Journal* in 1978, he praised Jack's abilities as a raconteur and noted that "some of Jack's favorite stories were passed along to him by his father."⁴⁵ Jack also retold some of his father's stories in his own columns, including one about an unfortunate encounter between a hunting dog and a skunk and another about a hog drowning in whiskey mash.⁴⁶ Jack quipped that they had a lot of time to talk because they spent so much time riding around in a car that only went twenty miles an hour.⁴⁷

In 1921, Gene developed a new interest: antiques (fig. 12). Andrew Sparks, an editor and journalist for the *Atlanta Journal and Constitution*, interviewed Ethel in 1976 and described the event leading to this significant development: "His life was changed the day a Mrs. Davis [probably Mary Lee Davis of North Milledge Avenue] and her daughter Caroline, who had opened an antique shop in Athens, came and asked if he'd repair old furniture for them. 'That got him interested,' Mrs. Thomas said. 'He started buying in 1921 and afterwards that was all he wanted to do. He could have made more carpentering than with antiques, but I let him do what he wanted to do.'"⁴⁸ By all accounts Gene had a singular passion for, if not an outright obsession with, antique furniture and the woods and craftsmanship that went into making it.

He found antiques, bought antiques, restored and refinished antiques, sold antiques, used parts from antique furniture to make new pieces of furniture, and made his own furniture in the style of the antiques he found. Jack explains, "Dad would buy lesser types of furniture and take them apart and produce finer pieces from them."[49] Regarding the fact that much of Gene's furniture was a mix of old and new, Jack writes, "He always said that if a reproduction was 75 percent old wood it was truly an antique"—a definition that allows for a lot of flexibility—and added that "sometimes he would hunt for weeks to find the proper old piece of furniture to have the right wood to finish a fine reproduction."[50] Even if it was not an exact copy of an earlier work, "reproduction" is the word Gene often used to describe the furniture he made. Many of the antiques he found required some level of repair, and most of the new furniture he made incorporated some older materials. His work as a craftsman and his work as a dealer (or "spotter" or "picker") were seamlessly intertwined.

In the early 1920s, a typical day of antiquing for Gene involved getting up early, driving his Model T Ford out to the country over dirt roads (repairing tires as necessary) and stopping at a country store to announce that he was looking for old-timey furniture that people had a hundred years ago. He followed leads to homes where he would again ask for the kind of furniture "your grandmother and mine had."[51] On a good day, he returned late in the evening with the car piled high with furniture. Jack, who often accompanied his father, albeit reluctantly, described how open everyone they met was: "These were good days because the country people would invite you into their home and there was never a thought that you would hurt them. In the mountains the people would look you over real close but once you met them they were very hospitable."[52] The next morning Gene's clients, whom Jack once described as "the affluent ladies of Athens," would come to his backyard to purchase his finds; some haggled and some did not.[53] In later decades Gene also sold some of the antiques and his reproductions out of his house.[54] His granddaughter Martha Puckett Roberts (Eugenia's daughter) describes the interior of the home as "forever changing" as furniture was bought and sold.[55] When Deanne Deavours, now a prominent dealer and scholar of southern antiques, visited Gene in the late 1950s as a college student, she purchased one piece of furniture he had made from his shop and another from inside the house.[56]

Gene traveled primarily within an eighty-mile radius of Athens, limited—at least in the beginning—by the difficulties of traversing

Georgia's rural dirt roads.[57] The towns he visited included Nicholson, Homer, Commerce, Carnesville, Maysville, Cornelia, Cleveland, Dillard, Tallulah Falls, Jefferson, Gillsville, Gainesville, Pendergrass, White Plains, Woodville, Crawford, Siloam, Sparta, Lexington, Union Point, Lincolnton, Washington, Elberton, and Madison. Occasionally he traveled as far south as the Augusta area and as far north and east as the Carolinas.[58] Possibly Gene tended to go south, where the wealthier estates historically would have been, when he went antiquing with other people and went north mostly by himself or with family members. Both Milton Leathers, whose grandmother Camilla Erwin went antiquing with Gene in the 1920s and 1930s, and Jack Rowland, whose father went antiquing with Gene in the 1930s, only recall hearing about trips south.[59] Jane Webb Smith notes in the exhibition catalogue *Georgia's Legacy* that much of the early furniture surviving from the area where Gene antiqued is from the Federal period and often has a combination of Federal and Chippendale elements, details reflected in the furniture he made.[60]

Lee Davis, a writer for the *Antiquarian* magazine, explained in an article in 1929 that the South at that time offered more opportunities for finding antiques than the North—where antiquers had been active for several decades—because southern furniture was just beginning to gain a level of appreciation and interest equal to that of its northern counterparts. Davis reported that hunting for early antiques in the South was a pleasant activity, "unencumbered by the commercial conditions usually attendant elsewhere [in the North]," and that "finds" were plentiful. Davis offered the following idyllic description of antiquing in Georgia and South Carolina: "it has become a social pastime among the younger people of these states to organize 'antique hunts' in which a party ranging from five to twenty people, embark on a tour via automobile, carriage and horse, for a period of a day or more. Usually a small truck follows them and gathers their purchases, which are invariably obtained at moderate prices and yield many excellent objects for the collection of the 'hunter.'"[61] Though not a wealthy collector, Gene was an indispensable part of such a scene in the Athens area, guiding many antiques aficionados on their trips to the country but rarely doing the driving himself. The individuals who went with him and bought antiques from him, though often of a different social set, clearly respected his knowledge of furniture and treated him as a peer.[62]

Davis's version of antiquing may have been similar to the trips Gene took with wealthier collectors, but the pursuits Jack describes often involved hardships such as freezing rain, dusty or muddy roads, and automobile repairs. Jack writes, "He would come in late at night, sometimes with a good find and sometimes with nothing, but the urge was always there to continue on the next day.... Most times he came in hungry because he wouldn't stop to eat. It wasn't a very good life, but it was the only life he wanted. To him, the next house might hold the fine chest of drawers or the Governor Winthrop [slant-top] desk, the high-legged sideboard or some other unusual find. He was as hooked as the old-time prospector who always believed the next hole he dug would be an El Dorado."[63] Gene went antiquing not as a hobby or a fashionable pastime but as a means of making a modest living.

Gene did not spend large sums on the furniture he acquired. According to Sparks, Ethel recalled, "The most [he] ever paid for a piece of furniture was $200," adding, "You could buy Winthrop desks for $10 or $25."[64] Many of the people he visited were poor, and the money he offered was welcome. Jack describes the poverty they encountered: "We went to houses that didn't have windows—they had openings with wood board shutters. There were always cracks in the floors and usually the front door was standing wide open. The chickens would wander through the house and sometimes get close to the fire for a little warmth.... I used to ask my dad how they were able to survive some of those houses. His stock answer was, 'They're tough.'"[65] Gene traveled a region hard hit by the Great Depression and the lingering effects of the Civil War. Deavours points out that the furniture he found often was damaged and worn, reflecting those hardships, but that he knew what it was supposed to look like and understood how to fix it.[66] Although Gene and his family were better off than many of the people he met in the country, they still had to make do with limited resources. Henry Green observes that Gene "had a large family that seemed to be sick all the time and . . . had a hard time financially."[67]

Gene was notorious in his family for his readiness to sell whatever was on hand for whatever amount he needed for his next purchase, regardless of the object's value or who owned it. Many of his family members have stories of his selling some treasured item belonging to his wife or one of his children simply because he needed some cash. Jack summarized his father's relationship with money: "If my dad needed a dollar to get a bit of shopwork done on an antique or to buy some hardware, he would sell the first thing that came to hand. The only value a dollar had was to help repair an antique or to buy one."[68] Jack frequently credited his mother with being able to help the family get by on what little they had and he described the division of their roles: "While

Dad was the artist, Mom was the business manager."[69] By all accounts, the furniture Gene sold was quite reasonably priced, and his grandson-in-law Frank Roberts (Gene's granddaughter Martha's husband), who enjoyed visiting him in his shop, explains that "most of the family felt that he charged about half of what he should have charged for the work that he did on a piece."[70] Arthur Kittle, brother of Jo Anne's husband, Richard, similarly remarks that "he could spend six months making something like a sideboard, and charge less than a thousand dollars."[71] Jack notes that his father "made several large Breakfronts of the finest types and his charge usually ran about a thousand dollars"; to emphasize how reasonable (or low) this price was, he adds that new, plain, white pine breakfronts without fine details sold for the same amount.[72]

When out antiquing, sometimes Gene would ask at the local store or the grist mill specifically about "the older families of the area," including African American families, because, as Jack explains, "Many black families had more antiques than the whites, because the whites would discard the old and buy new from time to time and the blacks would take the old home and use it."[73] Jack relates the story of one particularly memorable attempt Gene made to purchase furniture from an African American family:

> One day, Dad went hunting furniture and he wasn't gone very long. He came back home just burning up. He was so upset he couldn't work at all that day. We finally got out of him what had happened. The first place he stopped was a colored family's house, and out in the yard was an exceptionally fine mahogany tester bed. The children of the family were hacking on it with an axe. Dad tried to buy it, and the father of the children said it wasn't for sale. Dad said, "They'll chop it up," and the old man said, "That's all right. It's theirs." To my daddy that was the unforgivable sin. I had seldom seen him so upset. Every time he thought about it for years afterward he would get upset again.[74]

Though unsuccessful with saving that bed, Gene was persistent with his antiquing. If he could not acquire something the first time he saw it, he would remember where it was and perhaps try again years or even decades later. Henry Green describes one desk he bought that Gene had known about for twenty-five years before it became available for purchase. Green writes, "When he found out the people were ready to sell, he wired me in Birmingham that it was available and I came over with my trailer to buy it."[75] His persistence also paid off during one trip Mrs. Henry Green remembers: Henry and Gene found most of a slant-top desk in a house in Nicholson and, after some searching, discovered its lid being used in the corncrib.[76]

Gene's adventures finding antiques led to many such stories. Sparks records one in which he found a slant-top desk and, upon bringing it home, "discovered a lot of gold money hidden in a secret compartment," which Ethel made him return.[77] Sparks tells another story about a time when Gene "found a woman burning a four-poster bed under her wash pot," and when he asked her why she was doing that she replied, "'It's got bedbugs.'"[78] He also saw some unusual furniture; Mrs. Green says that Gene once told Henry about a sideboard with a table attached to it.[79]

The antiquing culture changed by the 1940s and 1950s, and the early days of riding around the countryside from house to house and filling the car with exciting discoveries disappeared. Later in life Gene visited antiques stores rather than private homes and in particular liked Noah's Ark in Abbeville, South Carolina (fig. 13).[80] His granddaughter Laura remembers driving byways with her grandparents and parents as a child on Saturday mornings to visit Noah's Ark. She thinks that the owner, Floyd Hawthorne, was a friend of her grandfather's and that Gene might have done some work for him.[81]

In addition to buying furniture while antiquing, Gene bought all the lumber he could find.[82] He also purchased "every boxwood he could get" and "would sell them to collectors to give an aura to the old homes."[83] Although it might seem like an inconsequential detail, his dealing in boxwoods hints at Gene's thorough understanding of the collecting market. The importance of the landscape to the overall picture increased as the public followed the restorations of the gardens at Colonial Williamsburg and similar projects. Gene did not simply provide attractive antiques to his customers; he helped them create a complete Colonial Revival setting.

Gene's customers included such prominent Athenians as Miss Otey Vincent, her sister Louise Dobbs, Camilla Erwin, Mrs. Ashford, Helen Bowden, Albert Sams, Pearl Wells Leathers and Fred B. Leathers Sr., the Creekmores, and Mrs. Hampton Rowland.[84] His customer base extended well beyond Georgia, though, and Jack writes, "He had buyers coming from all over to get the old furniture," adding that the Thomas family "would build crates and ship it to [customers'] home bases."[85] In particular, Jack describes a buyer who visited "twice a year from New

York and ... would stay a week ... to travel through the country to see items that Dad knew about but had not tried to buy."[86] Jack later writes that one buyer, a Mr. Kennedy from New Jersey (possibly the same individual), "never quibbled over the price of anything" and "bought practically everything [Gene] could bring in for two weeks."[87] Henry Green learned from Ethel, though, that Gene sold to northern dealers "with mixed emotions," suggesting a sense of allegiance to the South.[88] Sometimes Gene's finds reached their homes only after passing through the hands of multiple people. For example, Green purchased antiques from a dealer named Caroline Dearing in Chattanooga, Tennessee, who purchased them from a woman whose mother purchased them from Gene.[89] Also, as Deavours points out, Jake Bernstein, to whom Gene sold a lot of furniture, often sold to the dealer J. K. Beard in Richmond, Virginia, who in turn sold to the high-profile dealers Israel Sack of New York and Joe Kindig of York, Pennsylvania.[90]

In the 1930s, Gene continued to take others along with him on his antiquing trips, including Ethel, Jake Bernstein, Mr. and Mrs. Henry Green, Hampton Rowland, his brother-in-law Ernest Poss, Camilla Erwin, Lucy Redwine, and Mrs. Bolling DuBose.[91] When Gene went antiquing with Hampton Rowland in the 1930s, they always picked a pretty day and Rowland provided the car.[92] Hampton's son Jack recalls, "It was kind of a partnership. Anything that Gene really wanted he bought, and anything that Dad really wanted he bought and [they] kind of divided up the buying." Hampton particularly liked collecting and refinishing antique clocks, which he often purchased on their trips.[93]

When Ethel (fig. 14) joined Gene on antiquing trips, she focused on buying smaller items, such as porcelain, glass, dolls, and silver. Jack recalls that she "was always so proud of her finds, especially when they brought a good price," though he sensed that Gene was "a bit jealous" about her selling antiques.[94] Glenn Paul, who married their granddaughter Linda Martin (Mildred's daughter) and often spent weekends with "Granmomma" Thomas, laughed about stories of the couple competing for antiques. They did not buy items jointly—either he bought something or she bought it, and sometimes they sold things to each other. Paul adds, "If he sold something, that was *his* money; if she sold something, it was *her* money," and she would get cross with him when he sold something of hers.[95] In addition to buying and selling antiques herself, Ethel was a skilled upholsterer, caned chairs, and made and sold Raggedy Ann and Andy dolls.[96]

Fig. 14

Fig. 15

Fig. 14
Ethel Epps Thomas, ca. 1920. Photograph. Collection of Laura Kittle Hunter.

Fig. 15
Richard, Laura, and Jo Anne Kittle, ca. 1948. Photograph. Collection of Jill Kittle Thistle.

Jake Bernstein (1887–1962), who ran a successful furniture business in downtown Athens, joined Gene on some trips. By the mid- to late 1930s, Bernstein Furniture Company, Inc., included antiques in its inventory, and by 1947 Jake owned an antiques store called In the Ruff Antiques.[97] Jake sold furniture for higher prices than Gene and offered a fancier setting for shopping, a nice store on East Broad Street. Jack describes antiquing with Jake: "Mr. Bernstein disliked driving his own car so he would get one of his employees to drive for him when he and Dad went on a search for antiques. His cars were always fine, large cars so they could cover a lot more ground than a Ford." Gene taught Jake about antiques, and Jack describes Jake as an able student "as he was already in the furniture business."[98] Gene also found furniture that he sold to Jake to resell in his store and refinished furniture for him; sometimes, if Gene could not afford to purchase a piece of furniture, he would let Jake buy it in exchange for a finder's fee.[99] Henry Green explains that often Gene would sell furniture to Jake for a reduced price, if he could not get his asking price from his regular customers after a certain amount of time, because he "was always short of money and wanted to sell quickly."[100] Green relates one story in particular that suggests the volume of regional antiques Jake handled: in 1945, Green purchased Bernstein's inventory of antiques and promptly sold much of it, including *thirty-six* huntboards, before selling the remaining stock back to Bernstein.[101] Gene's niece Barbara Lumpkin (daughter of Ethel's sister Lourene), recalls hearing that Jake once offered her uncle "a lovely home on Milledge if he would work for him exclusively," but Gene turned down the offer.[102] Gene's grandson John Thomas (Jack's son) also acknowledges his independence, saying, "Granddaddy just wasn't the kind of person who was going to work for somebody else on a full-time basis. . . . He wanted to be his own boss."[103]

In the 1930s and 1940s, Bernstein Furniture Company periodically employed members of another family of cabinetmakers by the name of Thomas. George W. Thomas (ca. 1881–1971) operated his own shop on and off from the 1920s into the 1960s. Several of his sons, Lloyd T. (b. ca. 1905), Sidney Franklin (1907–1984), George W. Jr. (b. ca. 1909), Hubert (b. 1911), Herbert (b. ca. 1912), Jack (b. ca. 1920), Webb (b. ca. 1925), and Halton or Holton also worked as cabinetmakers, furniture repairmen, or upholsterers. Sidney Franklin Thomas later worked at the University of Georgia from the mid-1940s until he retired in 1975.[104] George's brothers, Jesse or Jessie Robert Thomas (1883–1969) and Jeremiah Cleveland Thomas (1891–1953), established Thomas Brothers

Furniture in the 1910s, which advertised antique and modern furniture, upholstering, refinishing, cabinet work, and repair. The company soon added furniture transportation to its offerings, which became its focus. By the late 1920s, Jesse and Jeremiah renamed it Thomas Brothers Transfer Company.[105] Though no familial connection has been determined between Gene Thomas and this family, they likely knew each other given their proximity and common avocations.

Gene enjoyed the company of people interested in antiques and working with wood. One of his friends was Garnett Doster (1891–1977), whom Jack describes as "a fine workman with woods."[106] Although the 1930 census lists him as a cabinet builder with his own shop, Jack Rowland remembers Doster pursuing woodworking in his free time. A friend of both Gene's and Mr. Rowland's father, Doster earned his living first by working at Moss Manufacturing Company and then at the post office.[107] His nephew-in-law Leonard W. Mize (1917–1989) also was an Athens furniture maker. Mize used traditional methods and both repaired antiques and created new works. He often made furniture based on photographs in antiques magazines brought in by customers.[108] Another local craftsman Gene may have known was Charles V. Staley (ca. 1876–1949), who ran the Athens Furniture Repair Shop in the 1930s and possibly longer.[109]

Although many members of Gene's family shared and continue to share his love of antiques, his influence on his son-in-law Richard Kittle (1923–2009, Jo Anne's husband) is of particular note. The Kittles (fig. 15) lived in a small house that Richard built in the Thomases' backyard for a while, and their daughter Laura was born there (figs. 16 and 17).[110] Later they moved nearby to 245 Boulevard (near Jack, who lived at 340 Boulevard, and not too far from the Puckett family, who lived at 156 Boulevard), and Laura considered her grandparents' house a second home.[111] When Richard joined the family he was young, a recent veteran of World War II, and became interested in furniture as a hobby. Richard's brother Arthur says that Richard and Gene "dovetailed" and that Richard learned everything about making furniture from Gene.[112] Like Gene, Richard made furniture using pieces of older furniture, for example a breakfront incorporating an antique Hepplewhite desk that he made for Mr. and Mrs. Albert Sams, with Mr. Sams designing the side compartments.[113] The Sams family owned the Coca-Cola bottling plant where Richard worked, and Albert Sams had a strong interest in antiques. Several family members recall that he was a great patron of Gene's as well. Richard continued to make furniture through the 1970s.

Another individual who sometimes helped Gene acquire antiques was Mrs. Cora Brightwell, widow of Dr. Charles Brightwell of Maxeys, Georgia. It was through her that Gene and Henry Green became acquainted (fig. 18).[114] Green rented from Brightwell while he lived in Athens and soon learned of her interest in antiques and that she occasionally lent Gene money to purchase furniture. One evening in 1936, Gene called her about some furniture he had found and Green ended up making the loan. He writes that, after they did this several times, Gene, whom he describes as "the most wonderful, unusual character," began to let him come on antiquing trips.[115] Green explains their business arrangement: "I would pay for it and if I wanted it I would give him a commission and keep it; if not, he would take it back to his shop until he sold it then refund to me the purchase price plus half the profit."[116] When speaking to the Williamsburg Antiques Forum in 1978, Green shared, "On these trips and in long conversations in his shop, he would tell me about the styles of furniture, types of inlay, woods, and how it was made. The dove tailing, mortise joints, saw marks, [planar] marks, nails, etc. He would show these to me on actual pieces. He also taught me how to examine a piece of furniture from the inside out."[117] After Green married (in 1939), his wife, Fran, sometimes would join them on trips. Mrs. Green says that Henry drove and Gene sat in the front and talked about antiques. Mr. Green's recollections support the fact that Gene was a storyteller, at least when the topic was antiques: "When he started telling a story of his experiences, he could not be diverted."[118] Mrs. Green reiterates her husband's view, saying, "he was a great talker and if you tried to interrupt him, no, he'd continue what he had to say." She also remembers that Gene's books on antiques were the first that her husband ever saw.[119]

After the Greens moved to Birmingham, Alabama, in 1946, and then to the country near Madison, Georgia, in 1957, Gene continued to contact Mr. Green when he found something he thought would be of interest.[120] Despite their friendship, Gene remained secretive about some of his sources. Green recalls, "Gene Thomas bought some items from a local house in Athens over a period of two or three years and, even though I bought several from him, he would never tell me where they came from." Green reasons that it was because sometimes people did not want others, especially family members, to know they were selling heirlooms.[121] Gene may also have wanted to keep some sources private in hopes of making future purchases, or he may just have been having fun.

Not surprisingly, one of the best-documented pieces of furniture by Gene is a mahogany breakfront (fig. 19) that he made for Henry Green in

Fig. 16

Fig. 18

Fig. 17

Fig. 16
Gene Thomas with his granddaughter Laura Kittle, ca. 1948. Photograph. Collection of Laura Kittle Hunter.

Fig. 17
Laura Kittle with an antique chair outside of Gene Thomas's shop, ca. 1948. Photograph. Collection of Laura Kittle Hunter.

Fig. 18
Henry D. Green, ca. 1980. Photograph. Collection of the Henry D. Green Center for the Study of the Decorative Arts, Georgia Museum of Art.

1950 that incorporates antique furniture. Green explains, "[I] bought an antique chest of drawers for use in the center" and "an antique wardrobe that was used in the rest of the piece." He described it as utilizing "old wood" and being "beautifully made."[122] The breakfront was the largest type of furniture that Gene constructed, and he seemed to treat Green's like a masterpiece given the scale, materials, and detail. The carving is extensive and reflects his finishing carpentry background in its architectural feel. The bottom section is set forward almost two inches to accommodate a chair rail, a detail often not present in manufactured furniture.[123] Gene included two labels on the breakfront, on the bottoms of drawers; Green added the date "January 15, 1950," on them and noted that the breakfront took six months to build (fig. 20). He also states in an appraisal that "a breakfront in American furniture is very rare," adding, "English examples are large and never appealing to me. I always wanted one. This piece was designed by Gene and me and I think it is perfect in size and proportion.... I think it will increase in value for its quality and beauty as the years pass. It's a very personal piece to me for the above reasons."[124] The Greens lived in Birmingham when it was made, then moved it to Greenoaks, their home near Madison, where Mr. Green displayed books and a collection of Royal Worcester porcelain in it. Green's breakfront clearly shows evidence of the reuse of old woods and includes old and new hardware. For example, some locks on the drawers are old, but the ones on the cabinet doors appear to be from the twentieth century and are marked by the Eagle Lock Company of Terryville, Connecticut.

Though he left Athens in 1939, Mr. Green continued to keep in touch with Gene and to buy furniture from him, remarking, "If I were within a hundred miles of Athens I would run by to see what he had."[125] He also took the knowledge that he gained from his talks with Gene and dedicated much of his free time to the study and promotion of antiques, in particular the furniture of the lower Southern Piedmont—the furniture that he had seen while antiquing with Gene. In 1952, Green helped with the first exhibition to highlight furniture from the South, *Southern Furniture, 1640–1820* at the Virginia Museum of Fine Arts in Richmond. Green ensured that Georgia was represented, and two of the works included belonged to Gene, a miniature blanket chest with geometric inlay and a walnut and yellow pine table (or stand) with horizontal bellflower inlay (fig. 21).[126] Jack later explained that the table belonged to Gene's great-grandfather, who received his weekly paper on it, and that it was made near Gainesville.[127]

In 1976, Green organized the exhibition *Furniture of the Georgia Piedmont Before 1830* at the High Museum of Art in Atlanta and compiled the accompanying catalogue. He acknowledges his indebtedness to Gene in the introduction, stating, "He is the man who should have written this book."[128] Green also notes that "the majority of the pieces shown in the exhibition passed through [Gene Thomas's] hands at one time or another."[129] As the first major exhibition of furniture from Georgia, it was a landmark event in the study of southern decorative arts, and Gene's influence permeated it. Almost half the objects in the catalogue are attributed to the Athens area, even ones that predate the founding of the town and ones that Green notes elsewhere were found in other towns. An attribution of "Athens area" may simply mean that the object was found by Gene Thomas within eighty or so miles of Athens. Those objects may have been made in the areas where Gene found them or brought there from the Carolinas or other locales as people moved to Georgia. Green included Gene's great-grandfather's table and the miniature blanket chest in the exhibition as catalogue numbers 59 and 93.

When looking through Green's catalogue, members of Gene Thomas's family sound as if they are seeing old friends. All the forms remind them of furniture he had around his home. One piece of furniture Gene made that has this familiar quality is the chest of drawers in figure 22. Prompted by his brother Richard, Arthur Kittle bought it from the Hamilton-Phinizy-Segrest House on Milledge Avenue, which became the home of the Phi Mu sorority in 1964.[130] The walnut chest has four graduated drawers with cut-corner rectangular string inlay, French feet, and fan inlay on the skirt. The legs and skirt are notably similar to those found on a chest of drawers illustrated as catalogue number 112 in Green's book.

While Henry Green certainly spread Gene's influence regionally, Mary Ralls Dockstader, a southern writer described in the *Atlanta Constitution* as "a charming representative of [Atlanta's] social contingent and the intelligentsia," gave him national exposure through articles she wrote for the *Magazine Antiques*.[131] Dockstader, who had a small antiques shop on The Prado in Atlanta's fashionable Ansley Park neighborhood, wrote two articles for the magazine in the 1930s that depended largely on her conversations with Gene. In 1937, she wrote about an itinerant cabinetmaker from Georgia named "German" Davis and relied heavily on Gene's expertise. She explains, "For most of the information I have gathered about this interesting figure I am indebted to Eugene Thomas, of Athens, Georgia, who has traveled the highroads and coun-

Fig. 19 Breakfront, 1950. Commissioned and codesigned by Henry D. Green (1909–2003). Mahogany, poplar, and yellow pine. 94 x 20¼ x 77½ inches. Private collection. Photograph by Michael McKelvey.

Fig. 19

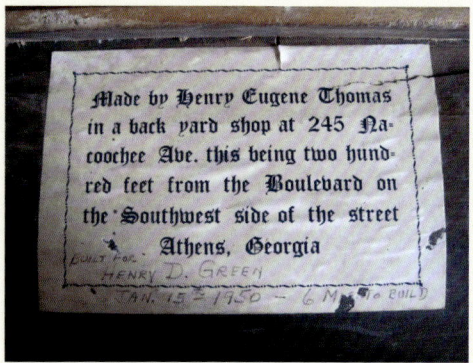

Fig. 20

Fig. 21

Fig. 20
Gene Thomas's paper label found in Henry Green's breakfront, n.d. Photograph by author.

Fig. 21
Unidentified maker (attributed to the Gainesville, Georgia, area). Table, ca. 1800–30. Walnut, southern yellow pine, and maple inlay. 29½ x 29¾ x 22½ inches. Photograph by Kenneth Kay, collection of the Henry D. Green files, Henry D. Green Center for the Study of the Decorative Arts, Georgia Museum of Art.

try lanes of the state for many years seeking antiques, and has found an almost unbelievable amount of good, and frequently excellent, old furniture."[132] According to Dockstader, Gene found numerous pieces of furniture in different areas that had remained in their original families and had similar oral histories of being made by a traveling cabinetmaker named German Davis. She writes, "Mr. Thomas at length concluded that he had stumbled on the trail of a peripatetic cabinetmaker who was working in Georgia during the earlier years of settlement."[133] While Green writes that Gene "knew nothing about the origins of the furniture he bought," because "only style, wood, and quality of workmanship" were considered important at the time, Dockstader's article indicates that Gene was aware of the history of the furniture he saw and noticed patterns in its provenance and craftsmanship.[134] The article illustrates several pieces of furniture attributed to Davis, including a sideboard from Gene's collection that came from the Booker family near Gainesville and a tall walnut secretary with an inlaid vine and heart motif and the initials "MB" for Martha Burns. The secretary, which Dockstader only tentatively ascribed to Davis, belonged to Mr. and Mrs. Bolling DuBose and is now in the collection of the High Museum of Art in Atlanta and recognized as one of the great examples of Georgia Piedmont furniture; its connection to Davis—and Davis's very existence—remains unconfirmed. Andrew Sparks wrote about this secretary in the *Atlanta Journal-Constitution*'s Sunday magazine in 1985. He reports that Mrs. DuBose told him that several people in Athens were aware of the desk and had tried unsuccessfully to buy it, including Gene Thomas, and that he took her and her husband to see it "way back in the woods of Banks County near Alto," where the owner finally agreed to part with it.[135] It is possible that Gene owned or found most of the furniture illustrated in Dockstader's article before it entered the other private collections she credits, those of Mrs. Willis Callaway, Mrs. Fonville McWhorter, and Mrs. Edward Inman.

Another important piece of furniture Gene found is a blanket chest now in the collection of the Georgia Museum of Art (fig. 23). Gene sold it to Jake Bernstein, and Henry Green acquired it when he bought the contents of Jake's shop in 1945. Green notes, "I had known about it for several years before that but it was never for sale," and adds, "Gene Thomas found it in a house north of Augusta."[136] Green included it in his book as catalogue number 101, and it appeared in the exhibition and catalogue *Georgia's Legacy* in 1985 as catalogue number 50. Although Thomas, Bernstein, and Green believed that it might be one

Fig. 22

Fig. 23

Fig. 22
Chest of drawers, n.d.
Walnut and yellow pine.
41¾ x 43⅜ x 22¾ inches.
Collection of Mr. and
Mrs. Arthur Thomas Kittle.
Photograph by Michael
McKelvey.

Fig. 23
Unidentified maker
(mid- to late 18th century,
lower Southern Piedmont,
probably Georgia). Chest
over drawers, ca. 1775.
Primary wood: red gum or
sweet gum; sides: poplar;
drawer interiors: oak; back:
southern yellow pine.
Georgia Museum of Art,
University of Georgia;
Gift of the Atlanta History
Center and Mr. and
Mrs. Henry D. Green.
GMOA 2003.6. Photograph
by Michael McKelvey.

of the earliest pieces of Georgia furniture known, dating to the mid-eighteenth century, current scholars believe it dates slightly later, to the last quarter of the eighteenth century, a date more in keeping with the settlement history of the area where Gene found it.[137]

Dockstader wrote an article in 1932 for the *Magazine Antiques* titled "Huntboards from Georgia," for which she also used Gene as a source.[138] The term "huntboard" identifies a tall, narrow sideboard, a piece of furniture associated with the South. Since the publication of the exhibition catalogue *Neat Pieces: The Plain-Style Furniture of Nineteenth-Century Georgia*, in 1984, scholars have moved away from using the term because it cannot be documented as period; the preferred terms are "slab" or "sideboard," which appear in old records.[139] The often-told story of the huntboard's origin is that it is so tall because it was used outdoors to serve hunters either standing or on horseback before or after a hunt. Dockstader's article, published in the preeminent antiques magazine at a time of emerging interest in southern antiques, likely added to the popularity of the use of the term "huntboard" among collectors and scholars. Dockstader quotes Gene at length when explaining the association of the form with southern hunters, bolstering his credibility by noting that his "acquaintance with the collecting byways of his state is exceptionally intimate."[140] Gene shared stories with Dockstader that he had heard about huntboards, including their role in hospitality and their location in homes, and noted that they often exhibited "crude construction" because their purpose "did not demand fine workmanship."[141] He states, "I have found more of them in Georgia and South Carolina than in any other of the Southern states. Some of them have a history extending over a period of more than one hundred years."[142] This is not the first published account of the term "huntboard," but it is an early one in an accessible and popular magazine.[143] The term quickly became ingrained in the collecting culture of the South. Interestingly, Ethel used the term "hunting-board" when Sparks interviewed her in 1976, though she notes that "people at the time called them sideboards."[144] The Thomas family still owns a piece of furniture that they call a "hunting table."[145] Given Gene's familiarity with the people in the country who sold him furniture and his interest in learning about antiques, it seems possible that he did hear the term from them when he first started antiquing. Regardless, it appears that Gene played a role in popularizing the term. Also, we can accurately use the word to describe the pieces of furniture he made and called huntboards.

Gene's shift from working primarily as an antiques dealer or picker to primarily a cabinetmaker was gradual. He focused on antiques in the 1920s and 1930s and by the 1950s he worked more as a cabinetmaker. Jack explained that "After antiques got scarce, he began making reproductions."[146] His grandson-in-law Frank Roberts, who joined the family in the late 1950s, noted that Gene's business as a maker was going full strength and he was antiquing less at that time.[147] Numerous antiques dealers, both companies and individuals, shifted to making period reproductions in the heyday of the Colonial Revival. For example, the Potthast Brothers of Baltimore originally bought and restored antiques but quickly moved into designing and manufacturing furniture influenced by their familiarity with the earlier works.[148]

Though much of Gene's furniture is difficult to date precisely, one of his earliest dateable works is the grandfather clock that stood in the front hall of his house (fig. 24). Gene promised the clock to Jack while his son sat and watched him make it in 1929; Jack in turn gave it to his son, John, who passed away recently and left it to his son, Sam.[149] The Chippendale-style mahogany tall-case clock has a broken-pediment bonnet top, four colonettes, a glazed door, ogee bracket feet, and works by Seth Thomas. Gene's granddaughter Laura fondly remembers listening to the ticking sounds of the clock mingle with the tapping noise her grandmother made while she worked on her upholstery projects.[150]

Another of Gene's earliest pieces of furniture, a cherry desk, also remained in his home, in the front hall, until Ethel bequeathed it to Jo Anne's family. Ethel describes it in her will as a Governor Winthrop desk, a Colonial Revival term for a slant-top desk. This desk is particularly well designed, with a serpentine interior composed of a central door over two drawers, flanked by two vertical secret drawers, and with three letter holes above two stacked drawers on either side. Gene echoed the curving line in the concave profiles of the letter-hole separators.[151] The desk has Chippendale-style brasses and ogee bracket feet. One curious detail is a series of small holes in the secret drawers on either side of the prospect door, which reflect decades of Gene poking them with various sharp instruments to pull them out.[152] Rather than adapting the attractive composition to make it easier to use, Gene likely copied an earlier design without making any concessions to functionality.[153] This desk made an impression on Henry Green, who contacted the family sometime after Gene's death to inquire about it and, upon learning that his granddaughter had it and treasured it, advised, "Well, don't let that go."[154] Arthur Kittle believes that making furniture like this desk was particularly appealing to Gene because he was interested in creating objects that people would keep and that would last a long time.[155]

Gene made another slant-top desk, of walnut with similar brasses, the same foot, and a different interior, for his sister Eula's son Morris W. H. Collins Jr. and his wife, Maysie Lyons Collins, around 1950. The center has two letter holes over two stacked drawers, flanked on each side by three wider letter holes over two wider stacked drawers. The drawers have flat profiles and the upper row is slightly stepped back. The dividers and the bottoms of the letter holes are incised down the middle and carefully mitered. Gene left visible the guidelines he incised on the sides while laying out the construction.[156] Both desks have large dovetails on the top, where the sides are attached. Another desk, probably from the 1940s or 1950s, with oval brasses with eagle designs and simpler bracket feet, also descended in Eula's family.[157] It has an attractive interior that includes rectangular string inlay on the drawers and a central prospect door with decorative oval inlay.

Gene Thomas, by all accounts an independent spirit, worked on his own schedule. He worked hard but not quickly. His grandson Jimmy Puckett (Eugenia's son) sums up his approach, saying, "'hurry up' was not part of his vocabulary."[158] Henry Green also addresses Gene's approach to prioritizing tasks: "I remember many times when we were talking, he leaning against his work bench, someone would come up and ask if he would repair a piece of furniture. He would reply, 'Lord no. I'm a year behind now.' Then if I suggested going on a trip, he would go in and put on a coat and tie and off we went."[159] Jack notes the amount of time his father would take on certain pieces of furniture: "He would work for weeks sometimes in building a piece of furniture because it had to have every piece of wood matched flawlessly and the dovetailing on the drawers had to be the very finest fit in the world."[160]

At the heart of Gene's business was his shop, a place that friends, customers, and patrons remember fondly. The first summer the family lived on Nacoochee, Gene built a small structure in the backyard, off the southwest corner of the house, facing the street (fig. 25).[161] Initially it served as a venue for him and his brothers and their friends, and occasionally the children, to play pool.[162] The walls still are marked with scores from pool games (fig. 26). After a while, Ethel got tired of their carrying on, and one evening she went to the back porch of the house and shot at the roof of the shop with a pistol. Jack recalls, "Men came out the windows, doors, and every way imaginable. Mom laughed and laughed about that."[163] Jack describes the pool games as "floating," moving to different locations as necessary, and explained to the current owners of the shop that the large window and lower wall on the south side of the structure were hinged (the window swinging up and the wall swinging down) to facilitate easy removal of the pool table.[164] This aspect of the building also would have helped, most likely, with moving large pieces of wood and furniture in and out. Once Gene became interested in antiques, the structure became his workshop.

The original room, which was three steps off the ground before years of accumulating dirt made the yard level with it, is about 300 square feet, and the two lean-tos Gene built add approximately 240 square feet.[165] The large front room stayed piled high with wood and furniture. Jack explains how his father's collecting habits led to the stacks of lumber: "Dad loved woods with such passion that it amounted to an obsession, and he wouldn't throw away a single piece of fine wood if there was a minute possibility of using it."[166] His granddaughter Laura recalls that there was just a narrow path, surrounded on each side by lumber, boxes of magazines and catalogs, cans of shellac, and tools, and that tools even hung from the rafters.[167] The back room, which housed a stove, was where he worked. His grandson John Thomas describes that area: "He had workbenches all around the wall, windows all around the wall and everything was covered in tools with C-clamps and coping saws, everything in the world like that."[168] Gene's granddaughter Susan O'Brian (Jo Anne's daughter) describes with affection the curls of planed wood everywhere.[169] Everyone acknowledged the shop's disorganized, rustic appearance and its ramshackle qualities. His daughter-in-law Hazel Thomas explains, "he never kept it in order. Just wherever he set it down, that's where it was."[170] In the summer he often worked outside, near a large fig tree, where he also sometimes placed furniture for sale.[171]

The shop made an olfactory impression as well. Henry Green describes it as "always [having] the strong smell of wood shavings, shellac, and hot glue," and John Thomas reminisces, "I just remember walking

Fig. 24. Grandfather clock, 1929. Mahogany. 93 x 12¼ x 19¼ inches. Collection of the Thomas family. Photograph by Michael McKelvey.

Fig. 24

Fig. 25

Fig. 26

Fig. 25
Gene Thomas's shop, 2011.
Photograph by author.

Fig. 26
Pool scores written in chalk on the walls of Gene Thomas's shop, 2011. Photograph by author.

into his shop you'd always smell the varnish in there. As soon as you walked in the door, it had a sweet kind of smell to it."[172] Milton Leathers was impressed as a boy when he first encountered Gene because even away from the shop he smelled of oils and wood—Leathers smiled at the memory and said, "He smelled good."[173]

Although at times children were instructed to stay out of the shop, it did have a magical attraction for some of them. Jo Anne's older daughters spent a lot of time there with their grandfather as they lived nearby. Susan remembers playing with her dolls in the shop while her grandfather worked and sometimes even being allowed to help him shellac or stain wood. She liked to pretend that she was his assistant.[174] Laura describes how his hands seemed especially big and wide, adding: "that was what I always focused on . . . , he just worked so rhythmically with every step that he took with his furniture. It was mesmerizing. Sometimes I would just sit there and watch."[175]

As Green indicates in the epigraph to this book, Gene Thomas worked in an old-fashioned way. Jack writes, "Dad knew all the tricks of the old time furniture makers and to achieve the beauty desired, he used them all."[176] Although electric tools were available by the time Gene was making furniture, he likely was more familiar with traditional woodworking methods and was not too distant from the practices of earlier craftsmen.[177] He did add a lathe and a bandsaw to his shop, but he preferred basic hand tools.[178] In one of his columns, Jack describes some of Gene's materials and methods: "The inlay in his furniture was done with a pocket knife and a hand saw cut off so the blade was only 4 [inches] long for grooving. Dove tailing he did with a hand saw and chisels. Smoothing was done with hand planes and sand paper. For years he used a hot glue made from cows horns and hooves; boy did it stink, but it would hold when it dried. The wood would break before the glue would turn loose."[179] Andrew Sparks reports that often when refinishing wood, Gene used "shellac, usually three coats, each one rubbed down with steel wool," and Jack states that "For securing the dull finish of old furniture he would use pumice stone and oil. Then a rag would rub in a soft sheen that was only available in one other way, by hand rubbing for many years."[180] Gene's construction techniques vary among objects, and his dovetails range from fairly fine to relatively unrefined. Frequently, he wrote on the boards where they were to go (e.g., "right inside," "left top"). Also, when his furniture incorporates parts of older objects, it sometimes shows evidence of more than one craftsman.

Gene's understanding of how wood worked impressed Jack Rowland as a teenager when his father encouraged him to ask Gene for guidance in his first refinishing project. Mr. Rowland tells the story of working on an antique huntboard that he still owns:

> That top is one piece of pine and it was warped up at least three inches and when I saw it I said, "My goodness! What are we going to do about this?" And Mr. Thomas said, "Oh, don't worry about that, I can fix that up. No problem at all." And . . . we took the top over to his house and Mr. Thomas shellacked one side . . . and took his garden hose and wet down the grass and then he laid that top down and said, "Come back in a week and we'll see how it's doing." And [when I returned] it had straightened back up just as straight as it could be and he let it dry for half a day and then he shellacked [the other side]. . . . he said, "You've seen what I've done. Don't ever wet the wood. You wet the grass and the ground and get the moisture, but you don't want to wet the wood itself."[181]

By all accounts, Gene had strong opinions about different woods. Jack writes, "The ultimate insult to Dad was to try to get him to repair a piece of furniture made of oak or poplar. To him, the only use for these two woods was on the back of a piece of furniture or as the sides and bottoms of drawers. The only woods worthy of his work were walnut, mahogany, maple, cherry, apple and occasionally rosewood. All the rest were so much crating and box material. For inlay, he wanted the finest satin wood."[182] Ethel reiterates his interests, noting that her husband preferred buying walnut, maple, and cherry (all local woods); did not like oak; and only liked pine in "hunting-boards."[183] She adds that he did not like pie safes or painted furniture, although Mrs. Green remembers that one of the first antiques she and Mr. Green purchased after they married was a corner cupboard painted black, which they found leaning against the side of the Thomases' house in 1940.[184] Gene also liked the simple, elegant lines of Queen Anne and Neoclassical designs. Those wood and style preferences, which he passed on to Henry Green, shaped collecting in the region for decades. It was not until the exhibition *Neat Pieces* in 1984 that a sustained appreciation for painted furniture began to develop.

One of Gene's primary sources of materials was old furniture, which he often disassembled to build something entirely or partially new.[185] One form he repeatedly repurposed was antique square grand pianos, which have thick boards that he used for library tables, his workbench, and his wife's pantry floor. Jack also notes, "Sometimes he would get a repair job on an oriental piece of furniture and he would use the ivory keys from the old pianos to replace missing ivory inlay."[186]

In addition to collecting and reusing old wood, Gene Thomas purchased materials from hardware stores and ordered hardware from catalogues. In the 1920s and 1930s, he patronized many local businesses, including Athens Hardware Company (fig. 27), Norris Hardware, Christian Hardware, the Dozier Lumber Company, and the Athens Lumber Company, where he had a lot of millwork done.[187] Jack records that his father sometimes had furniture legs cut or sanding work done at the Athens Lumber Company and that when his father sent him there on errands he always reminded him to request that one of two people, Roy Emerick and Roy Porterfield, do the work. Jack adds, "They would hurry to get Dad's work because they both thought so much of him. When they did a job it was done right."[188] John Whitehead, whose parents purchased furniture from Gene, notes that the Athens Lumber Company was known for its precision milling.[189] Gene's granddaughter Laura remembers going with him to Athens Lumber to get mahogany and light-colored strips of wood for inlay and that he would wait eagerly for the shipments of the particular mahogany he preferred (probably Santo Domingo).[190]

Laura remembers looking through the thick catalogues from which her grandfather ordered his hardware, adding, "He would have to order certain ones for certain pieces to make it look authentic."[191] Gene used Chippendale brass pulls and Neoclassical oval brass pulls with a variety of patterns, including an acorn, a sheaf of wheat with a scythe, a basket with a pineapple, an eagle, and a thistle (fig. 28).[192] His niece Betty Jane Gorham (his sister Ruby's daughter) remembers that he had various handles around his shop and sometimes customers could pick out which ones they preferred.[193] He used the thistle pull often, and Arthur Kittle recalls hearing his brother and Gene talking about how the thistles became hard to find. Richard often used eagle pulls, which were easier to acquire when he was making furniture.[194] Thistle hardware also appears on furniture made by Sidney Franklin Thomas, antiques that were purchased from Jake Bernstein, and other Colonial Revival furniture, including some made by the Charak Furniture Company of Boston in the late 1930s.[195]

Although no specific details are recorded about how Gene developed his designs for furniture, his grandson-in-law Frank Roberts remembers that he had lots of books on antiques that inspired him: "I've seen him sit down at the dining room table looking at pictures [of antique furniture].... Then he'd go out to the shop and build one."[196] Also, Gene's work was similar to the furniture he saw when he was antiquing. Frank marvels, "He could just look at something and rebuild it."[197] Laura remembers that he used pencil stubs to draw designs or make notes about measurements and other details on whatever was at hand—scraps of wood or bits of paper.[198] Much of Gene's work was custom, and Frank explains that occasionally he would go to customers' homes to measure where the furniture would go so that it would fit exactly. Martha Puckett Roberts remembers that customers often would see antiques that her grandfather had found and would request copies, sometimes with modifications to fit their specific needs and tastes. Arthur Kittle explains that Gene provided furniture to meet customers' desires, either finding what a customer wanted, such as an antique table of a particular size, or making it himself.[199] Also, if a family requested a copy of an antique, he would oblige. For example, when the Phinizy family requested that he copy an antique drop-leaf table so that two people in the family could each have one, he did so, and when the Hight family asked him to copy a corner cupboard so that they could have a pair, he did that as well.[200] Through this process of finding, modifying, and copying antiques, Gene Thomas absorbed the influences of the furniture he encountered. Although not all of these antiques were made in Georgia—some probably migrated here with their owners—they helped shape the furniture that he crafted, furniture that truly is a regional expression.

Gene Thomas made many furniture forms, including tables, desks, sideboards and huntboards, breakfronts, corner cupboards, chests of drawers, stools, clocks, cabinets, hutches, cobbler's benches, mirrors, drop-leaf tables, Pembroke tables, nesting tables, dining tables, and cellarets.[201] Even though Ethel was an upholsterer, it does not appear that Gene made furniture that required upholstery and rarely, if ever, made seating furniture. Most of his furniture relies on elements of Queen Anne, Chippendale, and Neoclassical design (more early Federal forms than later Empire forms). He combined elements from different time periods and sometimes added them to forms that postdate the style they evoke, a standard Colonial Revival approach.

Fig. 27
Athens Hardware Company, 480 Broad Street, Athens, Georgia, 1936. Historic American Buildings Survey, L. D. Andrew, Photographer. HABS GA,30-ATH,12-1, Library of Congress.

Fig. 28
Details of brass hardware used by Gene Thomas. Photographs by author.

※ THE FURNITURE OF HENRY EUGENE THOMAS ※

Fig. 27

Fig. 28

Several grandchildren recall that he made a number of sideboards, and Laura notes that she remembers those because "he was always fussing about that for some reason."[202] One of the sideboards Gene made was for Mr. Robert Watterson, president of C&S Bank in Athens, and his wife, who lived in a Colonial Revival house on Milledge Circle designed by architect Roy Hitchcock. The home, now known as the Watterson-Terry-Allen House, was completed in 1940. The Wattersons carefully filled the home with antiques, many of which were local, and Gene Thomas's sideboard would have been an appropriate contemporary addition.[203] This sideboard later entered the collection of Adelaide and Graham Ponder through their friend Henry Green. He knew that they were looking for a sideboard, and, when he learned that this one was available, he arranged for them to acquire it, probably in the 1960s or 1970s.[204] The sideboard has a serpentine front, six legs, light-colored string inlay outlining the drawers and doors, and tripartite oval stringing on the doors and drawers. Dale Couch, adjunct curator of decorative arts at the Georgia Museum of Art, notes that the design references both New York and Charleston schools, and that the tripartite inlay and flattened ovals are primary characteristics of Charleston's Neoclassical style, a logical influence on the furniture Gene would have seen when antiquing in the Piedmont due to the pattern of settlement from Charleston inland.[205] Gene made another sideboard for Martha and James B. Allen, a dentist, probably around 1950 when their grand Southern Colonial house on West Lake Drive was built.[206] Notable in the design of this sideboard are diamond inlays surrounded by rectangles, an extravagant combination that would not have appeared in period Neoclassical furniture.[207] Laura recalls another nonperiod variation of the form, a piece of furniture her parents had that was similar to a sideboard or huntboard but with a top that flipped up.[208]

One form that Gene made multiple times is a small desk (also called a secretary, desk and bookcase, or ladies' writing desk), and at least five survive. One of the desks, possibly the earliest, belonged to Lucy Leah (West) Mathis Redwine (1889–1965). Her son Bucky describes his mother and Gene Thomas as "big buddies," united in their love of antiques.[209] In addition to the many antiques she bought on their trips together, she purchased this desk and commissioned a pair of end tables as a wedding gift for Bucky and his bride in 1956. The desk is walnut and pine and, like much of Gene's furniture, incorporates reused woods. Though his granddaughter Laura remembers that he signed a lot of furniture in pencil, this desk has the only signature found during the research for this project; on the inside of the proper left side of the lower section appears in graphite, "Right/inside/made by H. E. Thomas" (fig. 29).[210] The two doors are glazed with an eight-pane pattern, the desk is covered with green baize, and the drawers have rectangular string inlay with cut corners. The Hepplewhite-style tapered legs feature Gene's distinctive bellflower inlay design, discussed later in this text. The top has large dovetails visible, and the shelves are adjustable. Couch notes that this desk form was not originally produced in the South often but became popular throughout the country during the Colonial Revival. The diminutive scale of the form would have appealed to a population living in the smaller homes and apartments common to the era.

Around 1935, Birdie Moss Bondurant Clower (1909–2000), a good friend of Gene's niece Marguerite Thomas, purchased a nearly identical desk (fig. 30) with her first paycheck from the University of Georgia. She kept it in the east parlor of the family homeplace at 725 Cobb Street, in Cobbham, an early neighborhood several blocks west of downtown Athens.[211] It has large dovetails on the top and uses the thistle hardware, which Clower's niece Mary Bondurant Warren believes would have been particularly appealing to her aunt, whose family had recently named two new roads cut through their property "Waverley" and "Windsor" after Sir Walter Scott's Waverley Novels and Windsor Castle.[212]

A few years later, in 1941, Gene made another desk, for his daughter Mildred, with several variations in the design. Rather than the eight-pane glass doors, this desk has a pointed arch design, with three arches on each door. Also, the bellflower inlay motif is slightly simplified, and the primary woods include cherry and mahogany.[213] No dovetails are visible on the top. This desk contains a rectangular paper label on the inside of the top drawer with a red double-line border and blue type reading, "MADE BY/HENRY EUGENE THOMAS/245 NACOOCHEE AVE./ATHENS, GEORGIA" (fig. 31). When Gene's daughter-in-law Hazel Thomas saw this desk, she asked him to make one for her, which he did, but with the same pattern on the doors and same inlay design as the desks belonging to Mrs. Redwine and Mrs. Clower. Hazel calls hers a "rainy day desk" because that is what Gene called it, though she is not sure why he did so.[214] A plain-style version of the desk exists as well, without the inlay and with wooden rather than glass doors, which Gene made for his niece Mary Alice Bland (1915–2000, his brother Tillman's daughter).[215] This desk, which has

Fig. 29

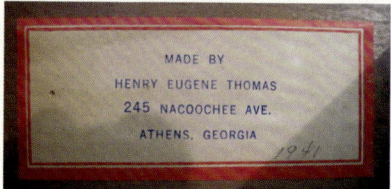

Fig. 31

Fig. 30

Fig. 29
Detail of the signature found inside a desk belonging to Morgan Roby ("Bucky") Redwine Jr. Photograph by author.

Fig. 30
Desk, ca. 1936. Walnut, poplar, yellow pine, and possibly white pine. 56½ x 36¹⁄₁₆ x 20¾ inches Private collection. Photograph by Michael McKelvey.

Fig. 31
Detail of a label found inside a desk Gene Thomas made for his daughter Mildred in 1941. Collection of Mr. and Mrs. Glenn and Linda Paul. Photograph by author.

slightly different proportions than the related desks, incorporates pieces of older furniture; the top half is a nearly intact element from an antique (probably northern), and the bottom includes parts of what probably was a chest of drawers.[216]

Gene's signature form was the end table, or two-drawer stand, with Hepplewhite-style tapered legs and bellflower inlay, and he often made them in pairs (fig. 32). He was making these by the mid-to-late 1930s, and they became especially popular in Athens in the late 1940s and 1950s as gifts for or purchases by socially prominent young brides.[217] Laura recalls, "It seemed like he was forever making pairs of end tables. Forever. I remember that more than anything."[218] Sets of tables and a few single tables survive in many collections in Athens and the Southeast. All the tables examined for this project are made of walnut and share the design features of cockbeading around the drawers, cut-corner rectangular string inlay on the drawers, and, of course, the bellflower inlay on the legs. They exhibit some differences as well, including slight variations in dimensions; variations in handle treatments, including the use of pairs of brass knobs, single oval brass pulls, pairs of oval brass pulls, and wooden knobs; and variations in construction techniques—for example, some tops are attached with a series of small glue blocks (a sophisticated approach), while others are screwed on and have simple screw pockets (a more expedient method).[219] Also, some have one drawer rather than two. The set illustrated is a particularly fine example and belonged to Gene's sister Ruby Parr, who used them in her living room on either side of a Victorian settee.[220] Her husband's name, Henry Parr, is written on a board on the inside of one of the tables. Like Gene, Richard Kittle made a lot of these end tables, whenever he could find a nice piece of walnut.[221]

These tables had many appealing characteristics that ensured their popularity. They were affordable, tasteful, classical, and identifiably local, especially because of the bellflower (fig. 33). Nancy Bentley Scruggs, whose mother, Emma Bentley, acquired a set of tables from Gene around 1936 for her home on Cloverhurst Avenue, refers to the upside-down flower as his "trademark."[222] Similarly, Birdie Clower's great niece Eve B. Mayes remembers hearing Birdie and her best friend Dot Firor describe what they called the "Athens Bellflower" as Gene's trademark.[223] His bellflowers are three-petaled, unshaded, single-piece forms below a diamond, which itself is below a pointed oval formed from curving lines that descend from the top of the inlay that runs along the edges of the legs. Gene's bellflowers have variations in their

Fig. 32

Fig. 33

Fig. 32
Pair of end tables, n.d. Walnut. 28¼ x 19⅛ x 16½ inches, each. Collection of Betty Gorham. Photograph by Michael McKelvey.

Fig. 33
Bellflower detail.

petals—some have large middle petals, some have tiny middle petals, and some have three equally sized petals. Although the bellflower was a standard Neoclassical motif employed throughout the country, the use of a simplified, single-piece bellflower inlay on Neoclassical forms does seem to have some historical resonance in the region, and Couch believes that Gene "was reviving a local tradition."[224] Certainly Gene was familiar with the detail, given that his family prized the table with bellflower inlay that Henry Green included in his Piedmont furniture exhibition (fig. 21). A similar table was in the collection of Florence and William Griffin, with a history of descent in a family in Habersham (now Banks) County, originating in the same general area of northeast Georgia as Gene's table.[225] Several other pieces of furniture with simple floral inlay appear in Green's exhibition catalogue, including a cellaret with a wavy vine and thistle design (fig. 34), which Green bought from Gene around 1945 and which is nearly identical to a cellaret from the Valley of Virginia illustrated in the book *Southern Antiques* by Paul Burroughs (1931).[226] Jane Webb Smith addresses the origins of many of these examples of Southern Piedmont bellflower furniture in *Georgia's Legacy*, noting that their influences derived from the areas from which Piedmont craftsmen migrated, such as Pennsylvania, Virginia, Kentucky, and the Carolinas.[227] It is possible that Gene found some, if not all, of the other bellflower examples in Green's book on his antiquing trips in the region.[228] The simple bellflower is a pleasing image, considered emblematic enough of the region to appear on the cover of Green's book, which in turn inspired the logo for the Henry D. Green Center for the Study of the Decorative Arts at the Georgia Museum of Art. Even if not all of the pieces of bellflower furniture that Gene Thomas found originated in Georgia, their longtime presence influenced and became a part of the visual vocabulary of the region, and the bellflower motif found undeniably local expression through the furniture he made.

In the 1930s, Mr. and Mrs. Green purchased an antique table, ca. 1800, with the same bellflower design and overall form from Gene, who found it in the Commerce area, north of Athens.[229] This table may be the prototype Gene copied for his most popular item. Mr. Green describes it as "unusual" and included it in his Georgia Piedmont furniture catalogue.[230] Unlike Thomas's tables, which are walnut, the drawer fronts on this table are crotch mahogany veneer, the top and legs are walnut, and the sides are maple; also, this table has a brass keyhole on each drawer. Henry Green's name is written in graphite in several places on the inside of the table, suggesting that Gene may have taken the table apart and marked the boards at some point after Green spoke for it but before he took possession of it. Though it is possible that Gene added the bellflowers to this table, given Mr. Green's interest in objects having original features he probably would not have requested such an enhancement.[231] Also, the inlay in this table is somewhat finer than that in Gene's tables, and it is unlikely that his finest inlay would be some that he added to an older table because it would have been more difficult to work with the dry wood.[232] Furthermore, though details vary among Gene's bellflowers, the juncture between the flower and the diamond generally is slightly imprecise, with the point of the flower not quite meeting the point of the diamond, while the juncture on the Green table is carefully and precisely executed.

As mentioned before, when working with inlay Gene used a customized saw (cut down to a four-inch length) to make the grooves and a pocketknife to make the curves and to add the flowers, which Jack refers to as "fleur de lys pieces."[233] Gene's passion for furniture extended to the details of the inlay, and Jack writes that "The inlay had to be a thin fine line of perfection, and he would not let it go until it was."[234] In addition to using inlay on furniture he made, Gene Thomas also added inlay to other furniture. Frank Roberts watched him add inlay to older furniture upon request, and Jack Rowland remembers his father taking furniture to "Mr. Gene" to be inlaid.[235] Though from a twenty-first-century perspective the practice of adding inlay to antique furniture seems somewhat improper, for Gene Thomas it was probably just good business. He made and sold furniture as his livelihood, so if a customer requested that he add inlay to a piece of furniture, it would have made sense financially to do so and does not imply any questionable intent. Deavours, who states that Gene "was a great decorator from an inlay standpoint," stresses that she believes he added inlay to older pieces of furniture simply to satisfy a customer's desire to make something "prettier" and not out of any desire to mislead.[236] His skill as an inlayer was so recognized locally that having furniture embellished by him might even have been a bragging point among his patrons.

Gene created several other forms closely related to the end tables, including cabinets that appear to have two or three drawers. The front of the cabinet in figure 35 falls open to reveal an empty interior with an opening in the bottom along the back, perhaps for electrical cords. Gene also made a coffee table version (fig. 36), which he codesigned with Marion West Marshall (1928–1964), probably in late 1957 or

Fig. 34
Cellaret purchased by Henry Green from Gene Thomas. Mahogany and southern yellow pine. 33½ x 24 x 19¾ inches. Collection of Mrs. Henry D. Green. Photograph by Kenneth Kay, collection of the Henry D. Green files, Henry D. Green Center for the Study of the Decorative Arts, Georgia Museum of Art.

Fig. 34

Fig. 35

Fig. 36

Fig. 35
Cabinet, n.d. Walnut. 29¾ x 23½ x 16¼ inches. Collection of Mr. and Mrs. Glenn and Linda Paul. Photograph by Michael McKelvey.

Fig. 36
Coffee table, ca. 1957. Codesigned by Marion West Marshall (1928-1964). Walnut, white pine, and yellow pine. 18⅞ x 17⅞ x 51 inches. Collection of George O. Marshall Jr. and Charlotte Thomas Marshall. Photograph by Michael McKelvey.

early 1958, shortly after she and her husband, George O. Marshall Jr., moved into a new home in Glenwood, a neighborhood southwest of downtown Athens, along the Middle Oconee River.[237] The couple married in March 1956 and received end tables by Thomas as a wedding present from her mother, Ruby Robison West, so the matching coffee table would have been an attractive addition to their furnishings. Marion probably took measurements to Gene to make sure the table would fit with a specific sofa and wing chair. She had the drawers placed on the short ends of the table so that they could be opened "without bumping into the knees of anyone sitting on the sofa."[238] Although some collectors of Colonial Revival furniture place the highest value on accurate reproductions of antiques, more idiosyncratic interpretations such as this cabinet and coffee table are particularly engaging examples of the style. Instead of simply copying antique forms, Gene Thomas and others like him adapted designs to fit twentieth-century tastes and needs and to express individual creativity. By the 1950s, many forms of mass-manufactured furniture with Colonial Revival styling were readily available, so customers purchasing objects made by Gene Thomas illustrates an interest in supporting a local craftsman and in having furniture that, because of its identifiable bellflowers and local woods, had a distinctly regional appearance.

Another related form employing Gene's bellflower motif is a set of nesting tables (ca. 1940; fig. 37) that he made for Dr. Thomas H. Whitehead (a chemistry professor and dean of the graduate school at the University of Georgia) and his wife; their house was designed in 1938 by Homer Nicholson, Mrs. Whitehead's brother-in-law, and is on Henderson Avenue, just off of Milledge Avenue.[239] They are made of walnut and have the finely tapered legs seen on the end tables. Each of the three tables has bellflowers on its front legs, so when stacked the group presents six flowers in a row, a veritable bouquet. The abandon with which Thomas used the classical motif and the form of the tables firmly place them in the realm of the Colonial Revival.[240]

A particularly compelling example of the Colonial Revival influence on Gene Thomas's work is a Neoclassical mantel clock, often referred to as an Eli Terry clock (after the nineteenth-century clockmaker), with a reverse painting on glass of Mount Vernon (fig. 38).[241] Few images evoked more patriotism during the Colonial Revival than that of George Washington's home on the Potomac River in Virginia. According to Glenn Paul, Ethel and one of her daughters, possibly Sarah, did the painting. They probably copied the scene from a print or another clock, as a similar glass tablet appeared on clocks by Seth Thomas in the 1920s and 1930s.[242] Their painting lacks the detail and accurate perspective of the source, but has a delightful earnestness. As with many of Gene's works, this clock presents a mix of old and new woods and old (the clock face) and new (the finials) parts.[243] It also has a variety of wood types, and Ethel told Mr. Paul that one of the clocks Gene made has approximately twenty different kinds of wood in it; he believes it was this one.[244]

Gene Thomas made a number of clocks, incorporating differing ratios of old materials to new. The Gothic Revival mantel clock in figure 39 has an old back, with remnants of the original Victorian paper instructions visible inside. Couch observes that the method of obtaining the arc at the top, a series of kerf saw marks visible on the back, though used in a few locales, is not characteristic of clock construction and likely reflects something Thomas copied.[245] Another clock of the same form as the Mount Vernon clock has an image of the Rocky Mountains (fig. 40). In the typical Colonial Revival practice of combining elements from different time periods, the popularity of the scene of the American West is much later than the style of the case. This object reflects a New England form filtered through a Colonial Revival lens and executed in southern woods.[246]

Another object that reflects the Colonial Revival's conflation of historical and regional details is the candlestand table in figures 41a and 41b. The heavy post reflects a regional vernacular treatment, and the more delicately turned elements of the birdcage are elongated, as if to emphasize the feature most attractive during the Colonial Revival. The carving is a rough interpretation of an early Empire New York waterleaf motif.[247] Couch describes this charming table, which also has Queen Anne legs, as a "mélange of anachronistic features." It remained in Ethel's possession until she bequeathed it to her grandson Jimmy Puckett.[248] Another tilt-top table that survives in the family features a similarly robust turned post, this time covered with bands of geometric inlay, and similar Queen Anne legs.

Although many pieces of Gene Thomas's furniture are not labeled and may never have had labels, the paper label that he used most frequently is remarkably detailed. It measures approximately 4½ by 3 inches and reads, "Made by Henry Eugene Thomas/in a back yard shop at 245 Na-/coochee Ave. this being two hund-/red feet from the Boulevard on/the Southwest side of the street/Athens, Georgia," in a black calligraphic font with a decorative border (fig. 20). Jack explains

Fig. 37
Nesting tables, ca. 1940. Walnut. 29 x 20 x 16 inches. Collection of John and Patricia Whitehead. Photograph by Michael McKelvey.

Fig. 37

Fig. 38

Fig. 38
Clock, ca. 1940.
Combination of woods including maple, walnut, and mahogany veneer.
29⅝ x 16½ x 4¼ inches.
Collection of Mr. and Mrs. Glenn and Linda Paul.
Photograph by Michael McKelvey.

his father's reason for the specificity of the location, "He said using the number of the house might be misleading since numbers are sometimes changed."[249] This detail conveys Gene's confidence in the longevity of his work. It also emphasizes the importance of place, of the shop itself, to his craft. When Deanne Deavours visited him around 1959, he made sure that she had labels (like the one in the desk he made for his daughter Mildred; fig. 31) to go in the furniture she bought. When asked why she thought he made sure she had the labels, Deavours replied, "He thought that it was very important that people know that he made them. And I think that was two different things: for one, he was proud of them, but the other thing is he truly . . . didn't want anybody to think that they were old and he was misrepresenting something."[250]

Several of Gene and Ethel's children exhibited artistic inclinations as well. Dorothy, Sarah, and Eugenia painted, and Eugenia, Jo Anne, and Jack wrote poetry. Laura says that her mother, Jo Anne, also could upholster and enjoyed restoring antique dolls. Jack made some furniture, including a huntboard, and created numerous wood carvings, such as walnut shells with miniature dioramas.[251] Several of the children also worked with antiques. Dorothy (who was a secretary in the fine arts at the University of Georgia) and her husband, Louie J. Pendley, sold antiques in the early 1940s and 1950s.[252] Jo Anne and Hazel, Jack's wife, ran the Calico Bonnet antique shop at the corner of Chase Street and Prince Avenue in the 1960s.[253] And Jack and Hazel worked in the auction business.

Jack's columns describe many day-to-day hardships the family faced, but he gives the impression of a close-knit family eager to laugh together and enjoy themselves. His writings also reflect that Gene and Ethel's life was not without tragedy. Sadly, several of their children predeceased Gene, and Ethel outlived all of her daughters. Many members of the family died of cancer: Sarah in 1947, Mildred in 1949, Eugenia in 1953, Jo Anne in 1982, and Jack's daughter Molly in 1961 and son John in 2011. Dorothy died in an automobile accident in 1969. Ethel passed away in 1986 and Jack in 1997. Many grandchildren and great-grandchildren as well as nieces and nephews and their descendants survive.

Gene experienced severely declining health during the last few years of his life. Several of his family members liken the symptoms he experienced to dementia or Alzheimer's, and Glenn Paul says that he was bedridden for several years.[254] Gene did not work much in the 1960s, and during that period his boxes of books and stacks of magazines, which he used as sources, were lost. Hazel Thomas and her son

Fig. 39

Fig. 40

Fig. 39
Gothic revival mantel clock, n.d. Unidentified mixed woods. 19 x 10⅝ x 4 inches. Collection of Mr. James Thomas Puckett, grandson of Henry Eugene Thomas. Photograph by Michael McKelvey.

Fig. 40
Mantel clock, n.d. Walnut, book matched mahogany veneer, probably maple, and ivory or bone escutcheon. 31⅝ x 17½ x 4½ inches. Collection of Mr. James Thomas Puckett, grandson of Henry Eugene Thomas. Photograph by Michael McKelvey.

Figs. 41a and 41b
Table, n.d. Probably walnut and unidentified hardwood. 30 x 23 (diameter) inches. Collection of Mr. James Thomas Puckett, grandson of Henry Eugene Thomas. Photograph by Michael McKelvey.

Fig. 41a

Fig. 41b

John believe that he threw many of them away and that no one found out until later.²⁵⁵ Gene Thomas died at his home on February 18, 1965, and is buried in Oconee Hill Cemetery in Athens. Jack commemorates his father in a poem titled "My Daddy":

> . . . . He was an artist at his trade
> and did the best he could
> he left no earthly wealth
> except his hands on wood
> his furniture graces the finest abodes
> and it shows his loving touch
> he traveled miles over the roughest roads
> to gather woods and such
> his artistry finally took its toll
> in his eyes and hands and heart
> God called on him for his soul
> and from us he had to part . . . .²⁵⁶

Jack's account of his father's view of heaven—"My dad always believed that heaven was a place where those who reached it would be artists at the trade or profession they followed while on earth"—emphasizes Gene's devotion to his craft.²⁵⁷

Though the shop suffered a period of dilapidation and Jack and John considered tearing it down, the current owners reinforced the weak areas and it remains standing. A few hints of its former occupant remain, including burn marks on the ceiling near where the stove was, a vintage piece of cardboard (with a pretty lady and the words "take it easy boys, I'm fragile!") used as insulation, the pool scores scribbled in chalk on the walls, and clusters of small holes of varying sizes bored into the outside of the doorframe, which Gene used to size dowel pins (fig. 42).²⁵⁸ The house has turned posts again around the front porch, and much of the interior remains unchanged. The "honeymoon house" and the two houses Nathaniel Thomas built still stand nearby.

Henry Eugene Thomas shaped the collecting and understanding of Georgia's decorative arts. He helped numerous Georgians fill their homes with fine antiques. He located several pieces of furniture now

Fig. 42
Holes in the doorframe of Gene Thomas's shop, 2011.
Photograph by author.

Fig. 42

Gene and Ethel Thomas, ca. 1920. Photograph. Collection of Jill Kittle Thistle.

prized by museums and may have been involved in the discovery of many more. He mentored Henry Green, aiding him in building his personal collection, teaching him how to examine furniture, and sharing his tastes in materials and styles. Because Gene's association with most of the antiques he found is not recorded, the level of his influence may never be fully realized. Because he used old woods and traditional methods when working on antiques and because those antiques now have had an additional sixty to ninety years to age, it may not be possible to determine exactly what repairs and alterations he made to them. For the same reason, some of his reproductions may be mistaken for antiques. Completely understanding what is original, what is old, and what is new on furniture Gene Thomas worked on and made will require extensive scientific analysis.

A letter sent to Henry Green upon the occasion of his exhibition in 1976 illustrates how quickly the history of the furniture Gene Thomas found can be lost. Mrs. George H. Corn writes, "I remember that Mr. Thomas helped my father find a cobbler's bench and he also made a pair of end tables for my parents. Mr. Thomas's name was a household word around our home whenever furniture was discussed so I imagine he was responsible for a great deal of the furniture I now own."[259] Only one generation later, just over a decade after his death, his involvement with specific pieces of furniture was unclear even to someone who appreciates antiques—a situation repeated many times and magnified over successive generations. Most of the individuals interviewed for this project commented on how much more information would have been available about Gene Thomas and his work ten or fifteen years ago. Much less would have been available in another decade or two.

The furniture Gene Thomas made stands as a strong regional reflection of the national craze for the Colonial Revival. He made some outstanding examples of Georgia decorative arts that look to an earlier time in the region's history but are completely of their era in their unique blend of old and new. His work also represents an important aspect of American craft: the individual working in his own shop using traditional methods. Deanne Deavours describes the pieces of furniture she bought from him as "perfectly proportioned" and "exquisitely done," and she describes him as "a real craftsman."[260] This exhibition is the first opportunity to see a large number of his works together and for visitors to the Georgia Museum of Art to appreciate his craftsmanship in person.

The research files for this project will be housed at the Henry D. Green Center for the Study of the Decorative Arts at the Georgia Museum of Art. Any additional information learned during the duration of the exhibition will be addressed in the publication of the proceedings of the sixth Henry D. Green Symposium of the Decorative Arts.

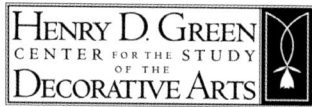

Endnotes

1. Henry D. Green, "Furniture of the Georgia Piedmont Before 1830," *Magazine Antiques* (September 1976), 551.

2. For in-depth studies of the Colonial Revival, see, for example, Alan Axelrod, ed., *The Colonial Revival in America* (New York: W. W. Norton and Company for the Henry Francis du Pont Winterthur Museum, 1985); and Richard Guy Wilson, Shaun Eyring, and Kenny Marotta, eds., *Re-creating the American Past: Essays on the Colonial Revival* (Charlottesville: University of Virginia Press, 2006). For more information specifically on Colonial Revival furniture, see David P. Lindquist and Caroline C. Warren, *Colonial Revival Furniture with Prices* (Radnor, PA: Wallace-Homestead Book Company, 1993).

3. Richard Guy Wilson, *The Colonial Revival House* (New York: Harry N. Abrams, Inc., 2004), 6.

4. Interview with Laura Kittle Hunter, by the author and Annelies Mondi, Jacksonville, Florida, April 21, 2010.

5. Marshall B. Davidson, "Those American Things," *Metropolitan Museum Journal* 3 (1970): 221-22.

6. Ibid., 223; and Elizabeth Stillinger, *The Antiquers* (New York: Alfred A. Knopf, 1980), xii-xiii.

7. Wilson, 7.

8. William B. Rhoads, "Colonial Revival in American Craft: Nationalism and the Opposition to Multicultural and Regional Traditions," in *Revivals! Diverse Traditions, 1920-1945*, ed. Janet Kardon (New York: Harry N. Abrams, Inc., in association with the American Craft Museum, 1994), 43.

9. For more on the history of Athens, see Frances Taliaferro Thomas, *A Portrait of Historic Athens and Clarke County*, 2nd ed. (Athens: University of Georgia Press, 2009); Frances Taliaferro Thomas, "Athens," *New Georgia Encyclopedia*, www.georgiaencyclopedia.org (accessed March 19, 2011); James K. Reap, *Athens: A Pictorial History*, 3rd ed. (Virginia Beach, VA: Donning Company, 2001); and Gary L. Doster, *A Postcard History of Athens, Georgia* (Athens, GA: Athens Historical Society, 2002).

10. Laurel Graeber, "Genuine Imitations," *New York Times*, October 6, 1996.

11. Rhoads, 54.

12. Jack Thomas, "Of Bird Thrashings and Skunks," *Athens Observer*, June 21, 1990, 9A. Contrary to traditional formatting, these notes include page numbers for some newspaper articles as a convenience to future researchers.

13. The 1900 and 1910 censuses list Nathaniel as a policeman; his obituary notes that he was a police captain during the tenures of Mayors J. F. Rhodes (elected 1902 and 1905) and William F. Dorsey (elected 1906, 1909, and 1914), and the local newspaper refers to him as Captain Thomas in 1911 and 1916 ("Appendix 2: Chief Administrative Officers, City of Athens," in Thomas, *Historic Athens*, 294; "Tribune's Tribute to Dr. Thomas," [Athens] *Banner*, September 1, 1911, 7; and "Mrs. H. N. Thomas Buried on Tuesday," [Athens] *Weekly Banner*, August 29, 1916, 1). Also, the 1916-17 Athens city directory lists Henrietta and Nathaniel Thomas as proprietors of a restaurant, the Boston Café, at 896 College Avenue. The [Athens] *Banner* reported that Nathaniel sold the establishment in May 1917 and intended to move to Florida, though he died in Athens several years later ("Harmon & Elrod Buy Boston Café," [Athens] *Banner*, May 16, 1917, 8).

14. "Captain Thomas Dies Saturday," [Athens] *Banner-Herald*, April 19, 1922, 3; Jack Thomas, "Life on 'The Boulevard'," [Athens] *Banner-Herald/Daily News*, March 10, 1979, 8; and Jack Thomas, "Sometimes the memory slips . . . ," [Athens] *Banner-Herald/Daily News*, January 10, 1981, Genealogy file for Thomas Family, Georgia Clipping Files, Georgia Room, Hargrett Rare Book and Manuscript Library/University of Georgia Libraries, University of Georgia. In 1904, Nathaniel offered for sale a pair of mules, wagon, and harness ("For Sale," *Athens Banner*, February 6, 1904, 6).

15. Jack Thomas, "Frozen pipes and frozen hands," [Athens] *Banner-Herald/Daily News*, December 31, 1983, 10; Thomas, "Of Bird Thrashings and Skunks"; and Jack Thomas, "I'll eat and talk like I want," *Athens Observer*, December 1, 1988, 21A.

16. Jack Thomas, "The good old days of moonshinin'," [Athens] *Banner-Herald/Daily News*, January 9, 1982, 8; and 1904 Athens City Directory.

17. Informal interview with Jim Trotochaud by the author and Annelies Mondi, Athens, Georgia, January 6, 2011. Trotochaud also recalls hearing from Jack Thomas that the shop once housed a still.

18. "Epps-Thomas," [Athens] *Banner*, December 5, 1907, 2; Hunter interview; and "Epps-Thomas," [Athens] *Banner*, December 22, 1907, 8.

19. Interview with Glenn Paul (husband of Gene Thomas's granddaughter Linda Martin, Mildred's daughter) by the author, Carlton, Georgia, March 23, 2010.

20. Thomas, "Life on 'The Boulevard'," 8; and interview with Barbara Lumpkin by the author, Bogart, Georgia, October 30, 2009. Around 1962, Hazel and Jack Thomas purchased the house at 835 Boulevard to rent it to students but sold it after deciding it was too much work (Jack Thomas, "The

Boulevard is regaining much of its splendor," [Athens] *Banner-Herald/Daily News*, December 20, 1986, 6).

21. Andrew Sparks, "Museum Harvest of Georgia Antiques," *Atlanta Journal and Constitution Magazine*, September 12, 1976, 18, general information file on antiques, Georgia Clipping Files, Georgia Room, Hargrett Rare Book and Manuscript Library.

22. Jack Thomas, "More on history of Boulevard," *Athens Observer*, December 31, 1987, 6A.

23. Jack Thomas, "The bells are tolling," [Athens] *Banner-Herald/Daily News*, June 11, 1983, 10; and Paul interview.

24. Jack Thomas, "The Story of My Dad and His Part in the Antiques Business," March 9, 1986, handwritten manuscript, collection of Hazel H. Thomas, lightly edited and reproduced in this volume (hereafter cited as Thomas manuscript); and Jack Thomas, "Ride Down Old Epps Bridge Road," [Athens] *Banner-Herald/Daily News*, August 13, 1977, 8. Following is a list of Gene Thomas's grandchildren: Dorothy's children: Anne Pendley James (1928-2006) and James William Pendley (ca. 1929-1994); Mildred's child: Linda Martin Paul (1948-2004); Jack's children: Mollie Melissa Thomas (1954-1961) and John Eugene Thomas (1953-2011); Eugenia's children: Martha Puckett Roberts (b. 1940) and James Thomas Puckett (b. 1943); Jo Anne's children: Laura Kittle Hunter (b. 1947), Richard Henry Kittle Jr. (b. 1949), Susan Kittle O'Brian (b. 1950), Russell Andrew Kittle (b. ca. 1961), and Wendolyn Jill Kittle Thistle (b. ca. 1962).

25. Jack Thomas, "Some changes over the years ...," [Athens] *Banner-Herald/Daily News*, December 27, 1980, 8.

26. Ibid.

27. Jack Thomas, "How to Eat Crow," [Athens] *Banner-Herald/Daily News*, September 4, 1976.

28. Jack Thomas, "Undercover man has yet to report," [Athens] *Banner-Herald/Daily News*, June 14, 1986, 10; Jack Thomas, "Old families ...," [Athens] *Banner-Herald/Daily News*, March 9, 1985, 19; obituary for Ethel Thomas, *Athens Banner-Herald*, September 2, 1986; and interview with Jimmy Puckett (Gene Thomas's grandson, Eugenia's son) and Martha Puckett Roberts (Gene Thomas's granddaughter, Eugenia's daughter) and her husband, Frank Roberts, by the author, Commerce, Georgia, January 21, 2010.

29. Gene did woodwork for at least two local churches. Jack Thomas reported that his father did "beautiful cut work that used to be behind the pulpit at the First Baptist Church" (Thomas manuscript). He also made Celtic Revival offering plates for the First Presbyterian Church. (Thanks to Charlotte Marshall, Tom Granum, and Gwen Griffin for sharing this information.)

30. Chuck Searcy, "Voters Will Determine Tuesday ... who wins," *Athens Observer*, September 11, 1975, 6.

31. Jack Thomas, "Time was, life was simpler ...," [Athens] *Banner-Herald/Daily News*, May 17, 1980, 10; and Jack Thomas, "Appreciating the Good Life in the City," [Athens] *Banner-Herald/Daily News*, October 2, 1976, 8.

32. Jack Thomas, "Make Me a Boy Again!" [Athens] *Banner-Herald/Daily News*, December 25, 1976, 4.

33. Thomas manuscript.

34. The Hardeman-Sams House, now an events facility, was built in 1910 by local architect Fred J. Orr and later served as the home of the WRFC radio station.

35. Thomas manuscript; and Jack Thomas, "The passing of an era," [Athens] *Banner-Herald/Daily News*, March 5, 1983, 8. Glenn Paul remembers hearing that Gene Thomas made a lot of mantels in Athens (Paul interview).

36. Tracy Coley Ingram, "Classic Places: Historic House Returns to Its Past," *Athens Banner-Herald*, May 17, 2000; and author's informal discussion with Janet Clark, Athens, Georgia, May 28, 2010.

37. Kathryn Grayburn, "Phi Mus to Show Restored House," *Atlanta Constitution*, December 1, 1966, 2, City file for Athens, Historic Buildings—Phinizy-Segrest House, Georgia Clipping Files, Georgia Room, Hargrett Rare Book and Manuscript Library; and Tracy Coley Ingram, "Classic Places: Home of Georgia's First Millionaire," *Athens Banner-Herald*, September 5, 2000.

38. William Mitchell's book on Neel Reid lists the James R. White Jr. House as by the firm Hentz, Reid & Adler with Reid as the principal designer. The job was number 319 and the job date listed is 1917, which may reflect the start of the planning rather than when construction began (William R. Mitchell, *J. Neel Reid, Architect, of Hentz, Reid & Adler and the Georgia School of Classicists* [Atlanta: Georgia Trust for Historic Preservation, 1997], 229). See also Charlotte Thomas Marshall, *Historic Houses of Athens* (Athens, GA: Athens Historical Society, 1987), 60.

39. Telephone conversation with Betty Poss (daughter-in-law of Gene Thomas's sister Bertha Poss), November 5, 2009.

40. Interview with Hazel H. Thomas (wife of Jack Thomas) and her son, John Thomas, by the author, Crawford, Georgia, December 1, 2009.

41. Lumpkin interview; Tracy Coley Ingram, "Classic Places: Talmadge House a Home Full of History," *Athens Banner-Herald*, August 1, 2000.

ENDNOTES

42 Barbara Lumpkin recalls her cousin Jo Anne hearing from her father when she moved to 245 Boulevard that she had a good house because he built it. Jo Anne's children never heard that he or anyone else in the family built it, but they were aware that Gene Thomas at least did some work on it at some point (Lumpkin interview).

43 According to the 1860 census, when Nathaniel was born, his family lived in the Tadmore District of Hall County near a chair maker, Wiley Rouse (1823–1887), who was born in North Carolina, fought in the Civil War, and moved to Alabama and then Arkansas; another chair maker living with Rouse named J. Martin (b. ca. 1836 in South Carolina); and a cabinetmaker named Jonathan M. Martin (b. ca. 1834 in Georgia). Though Nathaniel would not have known Rouse and may not have known the Martins, the census records at least suggest that older members of his family knew them.

44 Jack Thomas, "Songs and singing," [Athens] *Banner-Herald/Daily News*, September 29, 1984, 8; Jack Thomas, "The good old days," *Athens Observer*, February 27, 1975, 5; and Jack Thomas, "No football? UGA would dry up," *Athens Observer*, February 1, 1990, 8A.

45 Charles Salter, "Colorful Athens Man Likes to Spin a Yarn or Two," *Atlanta Journal*, December 21, 1978, Georgia Biography file for Jack Thomas, Georgia Clipping Files, Georgia Room, Hargrett Rare Book and Manuscript Library. For more on Jack Thomas, see the video "A Little Ghost Story," WGTV, University of Georgia, Athens, Georgia, 1971.

46 Thomas, "Of Bird Thrashings and Skunks" and "The good old days of moonshinin'."

47 Jack Thomas, "The yearly camp meetings," [Athens] *Banner-Herald/Daily News*, September 1, 1984, 8.

48 Sparks, "Museum Harvest," 18. Thanks to Eve B. Mayes for identifying Mary Lee Davis in an email to the author, February 4, 2011.

49 Thomas, "The passing of an era."

50 Thomas manuscript.

51 Ibid.

52 Jack Thomas, "Antique Hunting," [Athens] *Banner-Herald/Daily News*, May 8, 1976, 10.

53 Ibid.; and Thomas manuscript.

54 Interview with Arthur Kittle, with his wife, Virginia, by the author, Bogart, Georgia, June 1, 2010; and interview with Jeffie and Jack Rowland by the author, Athens, Georgia, January 7, 2010.

55 Puckett/Roberts interview.

56 Interview with Deanne Deavours by the author, Atlanta, Georgia, March 10, 2010.

57 For example, Jack explained that when he was a child, a trip to Atlanta from Athens "was a five hour ordeal," and that by the early 1930s "some roads had been paved and the trip took one to one and a half hours" (Jack Thomas, "You should count your blessings," *Athens Observer*, February 16, 1989, 9A).

58 Thomas manuscript; Thomas, "Antique Hunting"; Jack Thomas, "The 'old days' in Crawford, Ga.," [Athens] *Banner-Herald/Daily News*, October 11, 1980, 11; Paul interview; interview with Mrs. Henry D. Green, by the author, Annelies Mondi, and Julie Jenkins, Athens, Georgia, January 29, 2010; inventory made by Henry Green of the contents of his home, recorded by his daughter Julie Jenkins, 1987, shared with the author by Julie Jenkins; Rowland interview; Puckett/Roberts interview; Jack Thomas, "Of auctions, city hall and what not . . . ," [Athens] *Banner-Herald/Daily News*, March 31, 1984, 10; Sparks, "Museum Harvest," 18; and Mary Ralls Dockstader, "Huntboards from Georgia," *Magazine Antiques* (September 1932), 107.

59 Interview with Milton Leathers by the author, Athens, Georgia, January 9, 2011; and Rowland interview.

60 Jane Webb Smith, *Georgia's Legacy: History Charted Through the Arts*, exh. cat. (Athens: Georgia Museum of Art, 1985), 140.

61 Lee Davis, "Plantation Furniture: Georgia and South Carolina," *Antiquarian* (November 1929), 29.

62 Milton Leathers interview.

63 Thomas manuscript.

64 Sparks, "Museum Harvest," 18.

65 Jack Thomas, "How I Hate Cold Weather," [Athens] *Banner-Herald/Daily News*, February 12, 1977, 8.

66 Deavours interview.

67 Green inventory, 1.

68 Thomas manuscript.

69 Ibid.

70 Puckett/Roberts interview.

71 Kittle interview.

72 Thomas manuscript. According to the Consumer Price Index Inflation Calculator of the Bureau of Labor Statistics, (http://www.bls.gov/data/inflation_calculator.htm), $1,000 in 1950 is equal to just over $9,000 in 2011.

73 Thomas, "Of auctions, city hall and what not . . . ."

74 Thomas manuscript.

75 Andrew Sparks, "150-Year-Old Home for Georgia Antiques," *Atlanta Journal and Constitution Magazine* (May 31, 1964), in a copy of a scrapbook created by Mary Burdell with her father, Henry D. Green files, Henry D. Green Center for the Study of the Decorative Arts, Georgia Museum of Art.

76 Green interview; "Daddy's life as told to Julie in 1987, St. Simons Island, Georgia," a transcript of an interview of Henry Green by his daughter Julie Jenkins, which she shared with the author, 20; and Green inventory, n.p.

77 Sparks, "Museum Harvest," 18.

78 Ibid.

79 Green interview.

80 Deavours interview; and Hunter interview.

81 Hunter interview; and "Pictures from around the Town," website created by W. Marshall Leach Jr., a professor at the Georgia Institute of Technology, http://users.ece.gatech.edu/mleach/abbeville/town/index.html (accessed April 24, 2011).

82 Paul interview.

83 Jack Thomas, "Enjoying the birds and the boxwoods," [Athens] *Banner-Herald/Daily News*, April 25, 1987, 8.

84 Thomas, "Antique Hunting"; Jack Thomas, "Can you help us find classmates?" [Athens] *Banner-Herald/Daily News*, February 8, 1986, 8; Milton Leathers interview; interview with Nan and Fred Leathers by the author, Athens, Georgia, August 2, 2010; Rowland interview; Green inventory; Hunter interview; Green interview; and Thomas manuscript.

85 Thomas, "The passing of an era."

86 Ibid.

87 Thomas manuscript.

88 Green, "Furniture of the Georgia Piedmont," 551.

89 Green inventory, 11.

90 Deavours interview.

91 Informal interview with Karen and Bucky Redwine by the author, Athens, Georgia, June 21, 2010; telephone conversation with Milton Leathers, June 16, 2009; and informal interview with Morris H. Collins and his sister Margaret Totty (grandchildren of Gene Thomas's sister Eula Delceta Thomas Collins) by the author, Bogart, Georgia, June 17, 2010.

92 Rowland interview.

93 Ibid.

94 Thomas manuscript.

95 Paul interview.

96 Jack Thomas, "Ain't Mothers Wonderful!" [Athens] *Banner-Herald/Daily News*, May 14, 1977, 8; Hunter interview; and Paul interview.

97 Athens City Directories for 1938 and 1947.

98 Thomas manuscript.

99 Jack Thomas, "Our fine funeral homes," [Athens] *Banner-Herald/Daily News*, May 31, 1986, 8; Sparks, "Museum Harvest," 18; and Jack Thomas, "Our old friends . . . ," [Athens] *Banner-Herald/Daily News*, February 25, 1984, 10.

100 Green inventory, 2.

101 Henry D. Green, "Adventures of a Collector," a talk presented at the Williamsburg Antiques Forum in 1978, in *Georgia Inside and Out: Architecture, Landscape and Decorative Arts: Proceedings from the Second Henry D. Green Symposium of the Decorative Arts*, ed. Ashley Callahan (Athens: Georgia Museum of Art, 2004), 173–74.

102 Lumpkin interview.

103 Thomas interview.

104 Mary Bondurant Warren remembers that Sidney was the instruments man in the physics department in the late 1940s (email from Mary Bondurant Warren, January 16, 2011). Thanks to Nancy Scruggs for bringing Sidney to the author's attention.

105 Information about this Thomas family came from Athens City Directories, United States Census records, and advertisements in Athens's *Banner-Herald*.

106 Jack Thomas, "There will be no second chance . . . ," [Athens] *Banner-Herald/Daily News*, September 4, 1982, 10.

107 Rowland interview.

108 "Magic with Hammer and Chisel Turns Trash into Treasure," *Athens Advertiser*, January 13, 1965, 3. Thanks to Lucy Allen for bringing Mize to the author's attention.

109 Nan and Fred Leathers interview; and Athens City Directories for 1931 and 1937. The 1930 census lists Charles V. Staley and William W. Staley as cabinetmakers from North Carolina living in Athens.

110 Hunter interview. The Kittles' house eventually was moved near the intersection of Broad Street and Hancock Avenue (Puckett/Roberts interview and telephone conversation with Laura Kittle Hunter, June 14, 2011).

111 Hunter interview. Martha Puckett Roberts said that her grandfather may have worked on their house at 156 Boulevard as well (Puckett/Roberts interview).

112 Kittle interview.

113 Andrew Sparks, "See Athens' Classic Homes Next Wednesday," *Atlanta Journal Magazine* (April 23, 1950), 18 and 31. Albert "Buddy" Sams Jr. related that Richard Kittle made the breakfront for his father (telephone conversation with Buddy Sams, February 4, 2010).

114 For more biography on Henry Green see Mary Burdell, "Sharing Henry Green," 57–74, in *Georgia Inside and Out*.

115 "Daddy's life," 20.

116 Green inventory, 4.

117 Green, "Adventures of a Collector," 172.

118 Ibid.

119 Green interview.

120 Ibid.

ENDNOTES

121 Green inventory, 1.

122 Excerpt from an appraisal by Henry Green, October 18, 1978, shared with the author by Julie Jenkins.

123 Informal discussion with Dale Couch, Athens, Georgia, March 2, 2011.

124 Green appraisal.

125 Green inventory, 4.

126 *Southern Furniture, 1640-1820: A Loan Exhibition Presented in Richmond at the Virginia Museum of Fine Arts, January 21-March 1, 1952 under the sponsorship of the magazine Antiques, Colonial Williamsburg [and] the Virginia Museum*, exh. cat. (New York: *Magazine Antiques*, 1952), 46 and 60.

127 Andrew Sparks, "Ghost Haunts Athens Family," *Atlanta Journal and Constitution Magazine* (October 30, 1966), 30, Georgia Biography file for Jack Thomas, Georgia Clipping Files, Georgia Room, Hargrett Rare Book and Manuscript Library.

128 Henry D. Green, *Furniture of the Georgia Piedmont Before 1830*, exh. cat. (Atlanta: High Museum of Art, 1976), 9.

129 Green, "Furniture of the Georgia Piedmont," 551.

130 Kittle interview. Mr. Kittle believes that the chest of drawers stood in the upstairs hall. Richard Kittle likely knew about the piece of furniture through Albert Sams.

131 "Mrs. Dockstader Writes on Antiques," *Atlanta Constitution*, May 28, 1933, 9M.

132 Mary Ralls Dockstader, "Introducing 'German' Davis, Itinerant Georgia Cabinetmaker," *Magazine Antiques* (January 1937), 19-21.

133 Ibid., 20.

134 Green, "Adventures of a Collector," 174. Another indication that Gene Thomas was aware of larger patterns is Jack Rowland's recollection that he noted when a family broke up sets of furniture and could, for example, track down matching tables that descended with two sisters and put them back together, sometimes over many years (Rowland interview).

135 Andrew Sparks, "Extra Special: An Antique Mystery," *Atlanta Journal Constitution*, March 17, 1985, M29. Thanks to Dale Couch for suggesting this reference.

136 Green inventory.

137 Email from Dale Couch, August 30, 2010.

138 Dockstader, "Huntbords from Georgia," 105-7.

139 *Neat Pieces: The Plain-Style Furniture of Nineteenth-Century Georgia* (Atlanta: Atlanta Historical Society, 1983; repr. Athens: University of Georgia Press and Madison Morgan-Cultural Center, with a new foreword by Deanne Deavours, 2006). Historian and author John Bivins also addresses the issue of the term not appearing in period documents (John Bivins, "Hunting for the Huntboard," *The Luminary: The Newsletter of the Museum of Early Southern Decorative Arts* 10, no. 2 [Summer 1989], 1-3). Thanks to Sally Gant for crediting Bivins as the author of this article.

140 Dockstader, "Huntboards from Georgia," 106.

141 Ibid., 107.

142 Ibid.

143 Paul H. Burroughs included a section on huntboards in his book *Southern Antiques* the previous year (Paul H. Burroughs, *Southern Antiques* [Richmond, VA: Garret & Massie, Inc., 1931; repr. 1967], 61-62). Thanks to Linda Chesnut for suggesting this reference. Also, Dockstader used the term in 1931 as well for another article in the same magazine, writing it as two words, "hunt board" (Mary Ralls Dockstader, "Simple Furniture of the Old South," *Magazine Antiques* [August 1931], 83-86). The term "hunting board" appears in the *Atlanta Constitution* in 1928 and 1930 (classified advertisement, *Atlanta Constitution*, September 10, 1928, 15; and "Mr. and Mrs. Pund's Home in Akron, Ohio," *Atlanta Constitution*, December 14, 1930, 10M).

144 Sparks, "Museum Harvest," 18.

145 Email from Richard Smith (Gene Thomas's great nephew, his sister Eula's grandson), August 24, 2010. Thanks to Morris H. Collins for putting the author and Smith in touch.

146 Sparks, "Museum Harvest," 18.

147 Puckett/Roberts interview.

148 Catherine Rogers Arthur, "'The True Antiques of Tomorrow': Furniture by the Potthast Brothers of Baltimore, 1892-1975," 31-58 in Luke Beckerdite, ed., *American Furniture 2000* (Hanover, NH: University Press of New England; Milwaukee, WI: Chipstone Foundation, 2000). Thanks to Oscar Fitzgerald for suggesting this reference.

149 Thomas interview.

150 Hunter interview.

151 Couch discussion.

152 Hunter interview.

153 Couch discussion.

154 Hunter interview.

155 Kittle interview.

156 Couch discussion.

157 Email from J. David Smith (Gene Thomas's great nephew, his sister Eula's grandson), December 6, 2010. Thanks to Morris H. Collins for putting the author and Smith in touch.

158 Puckett/Roberts interview.

159 Green, "Adventures of a Collector," 172.

160 Thomas manuscript.

161 The 1913 Sanborn Fire Insurance Map for Athens shows a small structure in roughly the same location, so Gene may have adapted an older structure or its site.

162 Thomas manuscript.

163 Ibid.

164 Trotochaud interview.

165 Jack Thomas, "Buried treasure is around here," *Athens Observer*, November 10, 1988, 10A; and Thomas, "The passing of an era."

166 Thomas manuscript.

167 Hunter interview.

168 Thomas interview.

169 Telephone conversation with Susan O'Brian, April 3, 2010.

170 Thomas interview.

171 Green, "Adventures of a Collector," 172; and Hunter interview.

172 Green, "Adventures of a Collector," 172; and Thomas interview.

173 Milton Leathers interview.

174 O'Brian conversation.

175 Hunter interview.

176 Thomas, "The passing of an era."

177 Deavours interview.

178 Thomas, "The passing of an era."

179 Ibid.

180 Sparks, "Museum Harvest," 18; and Thomas, "The passing of an era."

181 Rowland interview.

182 Thomas manuscript. Couch notes that "apple" probably refers to birch.

183 Sparks, "Museum Harvest," 18.

184 Green interview.

185 Thomas interview.

186 Thomas, "The passing of an era."

187 Jack Thomas, "The hardware business in Athens," [Athens] *Banner-Herald/Daily News*, November 12, 1983; Jack Thomas, "History while city's still here," *Athens Observer*, July 23, 1987, 8A; and Jack Thomas, "A good word in behalf of the mayor of Athens," [Athens] *Banner-Herald/Daily News*, August 16, 1986, 4.

188 Thomas, "A good word in behalf of the mayor of Athens"; and Jack Thomas, "Memories of the old mill," *Banner-Herald/Daily News*, May 23, 1987, 8.

189 Informal interview with Patricia and John Whitehead by the author, Athens, Georgia, December 10, 2010.

190 Hunter interview.

191 Ibid.

192 Some of the retailers of reproduction brasses included the I. Sack Cabinet Hardware Company of Boston, which advertised in *Antiques* in 1932 acorn as well as pineapple and basket hardware similar to what Gene Thomas used, and Ball Brasses, which made numerous Neoclassical replicas, including a thistle pattern.

193 Interview with Betty Jane Gorham and her daughter Fran Gorham by the author, Athens, Georgia, March 16, 2010.

194 Kittle interview.

195 Informal interview with Nancy Scruggs by the author and Annelies Mondi, Athens, Georgia, August 27, 2010; and eBay auction for a Charak sideboard, item 150421723382, ending July 6, 2010.

196 Puckett/Roberts interview.

197 Ibid.

198 Hunter interview.

199 Kittle interview.

200 Informal interview with Ann Brackett by the author, Athens, Georgia, August 2, 2010; and email from Carol Dolson (Gene Thomas's great niece, his brother Tillman's granddaughter), January 19, 2011.

201 Informal interview with Carol Dolson by the author, Athens, Georgia, January 26, 2011; Paul interview; and Green interview. Gene made matching stools for his nieces Mary Alice and Marguerite (his brother Samuel Tillman Thomas's daughters), and Mary Alice's grandson Stephen McLeod recalls hearing from her that they cost five dollars each (Dolson interview; and email from Stephen McLeod, February 1, 2011).

202 Puckett/Roberts interview; and Hunter interview.

203 Email from Lucy Allen, August 27, 2010.

204 Informal interview with Adelaide and Graham Ponder by the author and Annelies Mondi, St. Simons Island, Georgia, April 20, 2010; and Tracy Coley Ingram, "Classic Places: '40s Home Mimics Colonial Revival," *Athens Banner-Herald*, March 6, 2001.

205 Couch discussion. For more on how settlement patterns affected the decorative arts of the area see: Dale L. Couch, "Confluence of Regional Cultures in the Savannah River Basin: Reflections of Settlement Patterns in the Decorative Arts," in *The Savannah River Valley to 1865: Proceedings from the First Henry D. Green Symposium of the Decorative Arts*, ed. Ashley Callahan, 51–71 (Athens: Georgia Museum of Art, 2003).

206 Telephone conversation with Nancy Allen, May 26, 2010.

207 Couch discussion.

208 Hunter interview.

209 Redwine interview.

210 The desk is in the collection of Morgan Roby ("Bucky") Redwine Jr. Thanks to Karen Redwine for her assistance examining it.

211 Email from Mary Bondurant Warren, July 25, 2010.

ENDNOTES

212 Email from Mary Bondurant Warren, February 1, 2010. The thistle symbolizes Scotland, Scott's homeland.

213 On this desk, the bellflower is directly below the pointed ellipse shape, without the diamond form that Thomas usually included.

214 Thomas interview.

215 Dolson interview.

216 Discussion with Dale Couch and Carol Dolson, Athens, Georgia, May 6, 2011.

217 Telephone conversation with Charlotte Marshall, October 27, 2009.

218 Hunter interview.

219 Couch discussion.

220 Gorham interview.

221 Kittle interview.

222 Scruggs interview.

223 Email from Eve B. Mayes, June 25, 2010.

224 Email from Dale Couch, August 20, 2010.

225 *The Best of Georgia: The Florence and William Griffin Collection*, auction catalogue, Brunk Auctions, Asheville, North Carolina, May 30, 2009, 37, cat. no. 0126. Thanks to Dale Couch for suggesting this reference.

226 Green inventory; and Burroughs, 82–83 and plate XVIII. The cellaret is cat. no. 86 in *Furniture of the Georgia Piedmont Before 1930*.

227 Smith, 141.

228 All of the bellflower furniture in Green's book is attributed to the Athens area, suggesting a connection to Gene Thomas.

229 Green inventory, 17; and Smith, 144.

230 Green inventory, 17; and Green, *Furniture of the Georgia Piedmont*, cat. no. 56.

231 Couch discussion.

232 Email from Dale Couch, August 23, 2010.

233 Jack Thomas, "The passing of the pride of craftsmanship," [Athens] *Banner-Herald/Daily News*, February 16, 1985, 10.

234 Thomas manuscript.

235 Puckett/Roberts interview; and Rowland interview.

236 Deavours interview.

237 Informal interview with Charlotte and George O. Marshall Jr. by the author, Athens, Georgia, June 17, 2010. Dr. Marshall believes that he and Marion had the table made not long after they moved into their home in 1957.

238 Email from Charlotte Marshall, July 26, 2010.

239 Whitehead interview.

240 Couch discussion.

241 Mrs. Thomas referred to this form as an Eli Terry clock in her will (Last Will and Testament [of] Ethel Epps Thomas, June 15, 1979, Clarke County Probate Court Records). Gene made another Eli Terry clock for Jack and Hazel when they married (Thomas interview).

242 Paul interview and see for example BANJO No. 5 - 1929, cat. no. 155 (vol. 1, 79), and BENNINGTON mantel clock, ca. 1932, cat. no. 2232 (vol. 2, 662), in Tran Duy Ly, *Seth Thomas Clocks and Movements*, 3rd ed., 2 vols. (Fairfax, VA: Arlington Books, 2004).

243 Couch discussion.

244 Paul interview.

245 Couch discussion. It is possible, of course, that this construction detail is from a part of the old clock that Gene reused.

246 Ibid.

247 Ibid.

248 Thomas will.

249 Thomas, "The passing of an era."

250 Deavours interview.

251 Jack Thomas, "The family grows smaller . . . ," [Athens] *Banner-Herald/Daily News*, September 11, 1982; Thomas interview; Hunter interview; and Puckett/Roberts interview.

252 Hunter interview; Kittle interview; and Athens City Directories for 1940, 1942, and 1952.

253 Hunter interview; and Kittle interview.

254 Paul interview.

255 Thomas interview. One of the latest dated pieces of furniture is the hunting table or sideboard owned by a descendant of Gene's sister Eula. Her daughter Gwendolyn wrote a note on it: "made by Uncle Shorty (H E Thomas) age 77, 6-60" (email from Richard Smith, June 22, 2010).

256 Jack Thomas, "My Daddy," from an undated and unpublished collection of poems titled, "A Bit of Love, a Mite of Sorrow, and a Smidgen of Levity," graciously shared with the author by Hazel H. Thomas.

257 Jack Thomas, "What Does 'Heaven' Mean to You?," [Athens] *Banner-Herald/Daily News*, November 17, 1979, 8.

258 Thomas, "The passing of an era."

259 Letter from Mrs. George H. Corn to Henry D. Green, October 4, 1976, Personal—Piedmont exhibit file, Green files, Henry D. Green Center for the Study of the Decorative Arts, Georgia Museum of Art.

260 Deavours interview.

GENE THOMAS AND JACK THOMAS, CA. 1940. PHOTOGRAPH. COLLECTION OF HAZEL H. THOMAS.

The Story of My Dad and His Part in the Antiques Business

Jack Thomas
March 9, 1986

Original handwritten manuscript owned by Hazel H. Thomas, reproduced here with her permission.

I have often wondered how to start this chronicle of my dad's life as an antiques dealer, and I still don't know how. I will just have to feel my way along and let the narrative explain itself.

Dad was a finishing carpenter at the time the antiques bug bit him, and from then on he was a hopeless addict to the lure of the fine furniture of the eighteenth century. He rode thousands of miles in every kind of weather in an open T-model Ford car, always searching out the cream of the craftsmen of a far past age. He would come in late at night, sometimes with a good find and sometimes with nothing, but the urge was always there to continue on the next day. Sometimes his clothes would be wet and icy cold from changing a tire in the rain of a winter's day. Most times he came in hungry because he wouldn't stop to eat. It wasn't a very good life, but it was the only life he wanted. To him, the next house might hold the fine chest of drawers or the Governor Winthrop desk, the high-legged sideboard or some other unusual find. He was as hooked as the old-time prospector who always believed the next hole he dug would be an El Dorado.

When I would wake early in the morning and ask, "Where you going today, Daddy?" the answer was always the same: "Where I can find real furniture, Son." Then he would say, "Today I will probably go down around White Plains, Siloam, and Sparta," or "up around Homer and Cornelia." Now, remember that all these roads at that time were dirt roads full of potholes and mud holes, and the Ford was stuck many times. Often it had to be dug out by hand when there was no one near to help with mules or another car. The Ford would only travel about twenty-five miles an hour so very often it was noon before he would reach the area where he was going to hunt for that day. The trip and the hunt were, more often than not, interrupted by one or more flat tires that had to be removed from the wheel, patched, and pumped up with a hand pump.

After the hardships of reaching the hunting grounds of the day, the quest would begin. Here came the real lure of the game. Dad would walk from the road to a house and when a lady or man came to the door, he would say, "I'm hunting old-time furniture that people had a hundred years or so ago, the kind your grandmother and mine had. Do you have anything like that?" Nine times out of ten, they would say, "No, we don't have any of that," but Dad wouldn't give up. He would ask them to let him see their furniture anyway, and he would explain that he paid real good prices for the kind of furniture he wanted. Nearly everyone let him in the house, and many was the time when he would come out the owner of one or more pieces of fine Sheraton, Hepplewhite, or Chippendale furniture.

I saw the old Ford come in many times with the top laid back so as to load on more furniture, chests of drawers and desks tied on the running boards and so loaded down it would hardly be able to move. The slightest hill necessitated the use of a low gear to keep it moving. When Dad came home with a good load, all the regular customers had to be called to come out the next day to see the goodies. Then the bickering would begin, and it was as much a part of the game as the finding of the beauties. A lady would swear that she couldn't possibly pay another dime over one hundred dollars for a piece, and Dad would swear that he couldn't take less than one hundred fifty and so on. Finally, Dad would come down to one hundred forty and start to walk off, and the lady would hastily say, "I'll take it, Mr. Thomas, but my husband will kill me."

One of Dad's buyers would come every six months for two weeks and never quibbled over the price of anything. He bought practically everything Dad could bring in. He was a Mr. Kennedy from New Jersey, and we had to crate all the furniture and ship it to his hometown. When he came, the whole family was happy because there would be lots of money for a while and the living was good. Most of the time it was a bare existence, and we never quite had "Easy Street" as an address. But then very few families did. We existed and had three meals a day even though it wasn't always what we wanted. Mom would buy a pound of cheese, melt it, and divide it in eight plates. This cheese, plus butter and jelly or cane syrup and homemade biscuits would be our meal. I could have eaten that pound of cheese myself, and there never was enough of it on my plate as I was a growing boy and perpetually hungry. The main thing was, we kept body and soul together—no matter that my pants might be patched and I had cardboard in my shoes to keep my feet off the snow. We were a family. We fought and quarreled among ourselves, but that was our way and we all loved each other.

 Mom would travel with Dad lots of times, and she would buy lamps, dishes, and silver when she could find them. She was always so proud of her finds, especially when they brought a good price. I remember one time Mama found a beautiful cut-glass coffee pot with a cut-glass holder so the coffee pot could be tilted on the two side pieces and poured without having to pick it up. It was a marvelous piece of workmanship, and today it would probably command a price of several thousand dollars. Mama had given a very small price for it; as I recall, it was only a few dollars. A party came by and offered fifty dollars for it, which percentage-wise was a very good profit. Mama didn't want to sell it, but Daddy insisted and she did. Even today, she still mentions it at times. I always believed Daddy was a bit jealous of anyone selling an antique except himself.

 My sister Jo Anne owned a child's rocking chair that was in my dad's shop. Sometime later, Jo Anne, her husband, and Dad and Mom were down in Crawfordville, Georgia. They looked in the window of an antiques shop that was closed, and Jo Anne said, "Oh, there's a little chair exactly like mine." Daddy looked around and said, "Was that your chair?" It turned out that the owner of the Crawfordville shop had bought the chair from Dad. Jo Anne had a fit, but it made no difference. The chair was gone.

 I had, at one time, a beautiful Kentucky rifle with an octagon barrel and curly maple stock with German silver inlay all over it and a silver patch box in the stock. I came home one time and asked Mama where my rifle was and she said, "Your daddy sold it for a dollar." My footprints must still be on the walls of the house. I didn't have one fit; I had several. That gun is now pictured in a gun book I have, and the price tag is $3,500. If my dad needed a dollar to get a bit of shop-work done on an antique or to buy some hardware, he would sell the first thing that came to hand. The only value a dollar had was to help repair an antique or to buy one. If the family had enough rags to cover nakedness and a little food to eat, then money went for more antiques or to the search for them.

In between trips to the country, Dad would reproduce the finest furniture ever made. He would buy lesser furniture sometimes, take the best wood out of it, and incorporate that wood into a special breakfront, sideboard, or desk. His work was exceptionally beautiful because he was a true artist at his trade. He would work for weeks sometimes in building a piece of furniture because it had to have every piece of wood matched flawlessly and the dovetailing on the drawers had to be the very finest fit in the world. The inlay had to be a thin fine line of perfection, and he would not let it go until it was.

I have called many people who have bought furniture that my dad made and tried to buy it back, but invariably I get the same answer: "Do you think we're crazy? No, you can't buy it. It's not for sale at any price." This answer, of course, makes me very proud of Dad, but then I would like to have a few more pieces he made. We have a one-drawer maple sewing table, two inlaid two-drawer sewing tables made of walnut, a beautiful inlaid "rainy day desk," and an Eli Terry clock he reproduced. They are all masterpieces. It doesn't take an expert to see that these were made by a master craftsman. He would sometimes reproduce a six-legged serpentine-front sideboard complete with inlay and the decanter bottle drawers, all so finely finished they were like a fine painting, to be admired but not used.

The ultimate insult to Dad was to try to get him to repair a piece of furniture made of oak or poplar. To him, the only use for these two woods was on the back of a piece of furniture or as the sides and bottoms of drawers. The only woods worthy of his work were walnut, mahogany, maple, cherry, apple and occasionally rosewood. All the rest were so much crating and box material. For inlay, he wanted the finest satin wood.

He made several large breakfronts of the finest types and his charge usually ran about a thousand dollars at a time when white pine breakfronts newly made were bringing the same price. His had crotched mahogany fronts on the drawers, solid mahogany doors with thirteen-pane glass, and the finest interior on the desk part of the piece.

One day, Mrs. B. F. Hardeman came to Dad and asked him to build four mantels for her house (now the offices and studios of radio station WRFC). She wanted the finest patterns available, with sunburst carvings in the middle and one on each side leg or standard. Dad set to work and carved the sunbursts by hand. He put the mantels together and then added the most beautiful moldings. Mrs. Hardeman was thrilled to no end with them when they were set.

A few years later, she left Athens to live in Atlanta with her sister Mrs. Inman. When she left, she called Dad out to her house and gave him her late husband's checkerboard for me. I still have it, and it is a beautiful piece of work, with oak leaves and acorns burned in the wood around the squares and the initials B. F. H. burned into the back of it. He was the same Frank Hardeman for whom the Demolay Chapter in Athens is named. But to get back to those mantels. One night I went to town to mail some letters and stopped off at a café to get a cup of coffee. This was about 3 a.m. and L. H.

Christian, then the owner of WRFC, came in. He and I were sitting there talking, and he mentioned about buying a house on Milledge Avenue for his studios. He said, "Jack, I wish you could see those mantels in that house. They are perfectly beautiful. Come on and let's ride out there and see them. I would give a lot to know who made them." When we got to the house, I recognized it immediately, and when we went inside I said, "L. H., you don't have to give anything to know. My daddy made these in 1922 and installed them for Mrs. Hardeman." He was really surprised, but he is still proud of those mantels. Two of them had to be removed to make way for his equipment, but the two downstairs are a fine feature of the front offices.

 When I was very young, I learned to love books and read everything I could lay my hands on. Now we had no public libraries, so my friends and I would scrounge books from anywhere we could and swap them back and forth. About the time I learned to understand more of what I was reading, Mr. James White built a fine home on the corner of Prince and Nacoochee, and Dad worked on that job as a carpenter. When the house was finished, Mr. White moved his library in first, and Dad was still working on the fine trim. I would go with him every day and read as fast as I could to finish a book. This was a part of my education, and I don't think Mr. White ever realized how much I enjoyed Dad working on his house.

 When Dad did carpentry work, it was always his job to stay on after the usual run of the mill work and finish up the fine bookshelves, picture moldings, and the intricate dentil work that went into making a fine house a superb mansion. The beautiful cut work that used to be behind the pulpit at the First Baptist Church here in Athens was the result of his artistry. I think it has been mostly removed in later years, but it was lovely while it lasted.

Dad loved woods with such passion that it amounted to an obsession, and he wouldn't throw away a single piece of fine wood if there was a minute possibility of using it. One time in later years while I was in the construction business, I sent my carpenters out to our house to repair the back porch. They needed a two by four to finish, so they looked under the house and found a mahogany two by four that Dad had bought for table legs. Not knowing woods, they nailed it up. When I went out to inspect the work, I turned white and said, "Good gracious, get that two by four out of there before Dad sees it or he'll kill us all." Hell never had the fury my dad had at the ruining of a piece of fine wood.

One day, Dad went hunting furniture and he wasn't gone very long. He came back home just burning up. He was so upset he couldn't work at all that day. We finally got out of him what had happened. The first place he stopped was a colored family's house, and out in the yard was an exceptionally fine mahogany tester bed. The children of the family were hacking on it with an axe. Dad tried to buy it, and the father of the children said it wasn't for sale. Dad said, "They'll chop it up," and the old man said, "That's all right. It's theirs." To my daddy that was the unforgivable sin. I had seldom seen him so upset. Every time he thought about it for years afterward he would get upset again.

One afternoon late, Dad and Mom and my sister were working houses on Morton Road, which was a dirt road at that time, and it was well after dark when they started home. When they reached Lexington Road, Dad didn't see it and went straight into Mr. Robert Hardman's filling station, knocking down one of the twelve-by-twelve timbers holding up the shed over the gas tanks. It nearly scared Mama and my sister to death but not Dad. He told Mr. Hardman that he would be back the next day to replace the column and cranked up his old Ford and came on home. It took him all the next day to repair the damage to the station, but the Ford wasn't hurt. Those old cars were sturdy, and you had to work at it to destroy one of them. We never had one that looked nice for more than three or four days because Dad would always tear the back of the body off and build a flat truck bed to haul furniture. One time, in 1926, he decided to trade his Ford out because the one he had leaked water and ran hot. He found a beautiful 1923 sedan in Homer, Georgia, and it was perfect. It was clean as a pin, with glass windows to keep out the cold, and the motor ran like the proverbial sewing machine. When he came home with that Ford, there was rejoicing in the house. We had a nice car at last. Our joy was short lived, however, for in about three days Dad had torn all the body from the back of the front seat off and had a flat bed there. There was a weeping and wailing that he had destroyed the best car we had ever owned. I was eleven years old at that time and had been driving alone for a year. I had had visions of riding around in that fine sedan impressing everyone with our wealth that we could own so fine a car. But that was my Dad. If he couldn't haul furniture on it, it was useless.

 One time, Dad bought so much furniture he couldn't bring it all in on the Ford, so he borrowed a trailer from my late brother-in-law Louie J. Pendley. We tied the trailer on the back of the Ford and headed out toward Jefferson, Georgia. At that time, Jefferson Road was only paved for a short distance, and when we hit the corduroyed dirt road the baling wire we had the trailer tied on with broke. I noticed something passing us out of the corner of my eye, then did a double take. That trailer was running up the road faster than we were and passing as it should on the left. I slowed down and watched it go on up the road for about a hundred yards or so until it went into a ditch. We got it out, and this time we tied it with a rope. We went on to Jefferson, loaded the Ford and the trailer, and came on home with no more trouble.

Mom and my older sisters wanted to go to Atlanta to see friends one time, so they talked Dad into staying home a day so they could use the car. At that time, we had a touring car and the top would fold back so Dad hadn't torn it off. He would just fold it back and pile furniture as high as possible on it. Mom got her brother Robert Epps to drive them to Atlanta. Dad told them the horn didn't work and they had better be careful. The morning they were to leave we got up about five o'clock, and Robert showed up carrying a bugle. Nearly all the roads to Atlanta in 1923 were dirt and so in a T-model Ford it was about a five-hour trip. When they got back that night, they were all laughing their heads off. They said when they pulled up behind a car Robert would sound off on that bugle and the other driver would nearly wreck getting out of the way.

One time Mom and Dad were in the country buying furniture; they had it tied on both running boards and piled on the back seat as high as possible. At that time in the early 1920s, medicine shows were traveling all over the South and when Mom and Dad pulled into a small town and Dad got out to see if a house had any antiques, a small boy rode up on a bicycle and asked, "Lady, are you all going to show here tonight?" I don't think Mom ever got over that.

My dad didn't believe any other car would traverse the country he traveled except the T-model Ford, which was the most cantankerous beast in the world at times and would have tried the patience of Job. Many mornings, I would have to go into the backyard and help Dad crank the old Ford to start on the day's work. I would turn on the switch and pull out the choke and retard the spark (to keep the Ford from kicking), and he would turn the crank. Many arms were broken by the kick of a T-model.

One cold morning, Dad and I worked long and hard to crank the car; it was really stubborn and wouldn't crank no matter what we did. We cleaned all the points on the spark coils, dried all the dew off the spark plugs, and drained the water from the radiator and replaced it with hot water, and it still wouldn't crank. Finally, Dad became so exasperated he grabbed a board off the ground, said, "Dern you! You will crank!" and slammed the board down across the tie rods that braced the radiator to the dash. Well, believe it or not, the old Ford cranked up by itself. I flew into the house and fell out on the floor laughing because it was so funny. I didn't dare laugh in the yard because as angry as he was he would have hit me with that board. When I told Mama and my sisters what had happened they fell out laughing and when Dad came into the house we were all rolling on the floor. He couldn't be mad then as he saw the humor of it all, and that whole day was happier for us all because of it.

The old Ford was a pleasure to own because anyone could drive or repair it, and it seldom needed anything drastic done to it. The motor could be overhauled in less than a day, and the reverse, low gear, and brakes were no problem for anyone to repair. A standing joke of the era was that a preacher named Billy Sunday died and went to heaven, where Saint Peter showed him a small shack that was his eternal home. Billy looked at a large mansion on the hill and asked who that belonged to, and Saint Peter told him it was Henry Ford's future home. When Billy asked why, Saint Peter said it was because he shook the hell out of more people than you ever preached out of them. As I said, it was a cantankerous beast, but it did its job in a way that no other vehicle could have done, and that malodorous, conniving scoundrel carried me and Dad many a mile and hauled many fine pieces of furniture in rain, sleet, snow, and sunshine. It did the job that was to be done and did it economically, which is more than I can say about any vehicle today. When Henry changed to the B and A models, the world lost a friend, and since that time they haven't had one quite so true or inexpensive. Many's the time I have heard people say, "I would give a lot for a T-model Ford." They were dependable and would get you where you were going and back, even if you might have to stop sometimes and throw a handful of sand into the transmission so it would grab hold and go. Many's the time I stopped in the road and picked up horse manure to put in the radiator to stop the leaks, and sometimes we would stop and get a gallon of kerosene to take us far enough to get gas to continue on our journey. Yes, the old Ford would run on kerosene for a short journey, but it would run hotter than usual and you had to get regular gasoline as quick as you could.

The T-model got around twenty-five to thirty miles to a gallon of gas, and on Sundays we kids would gather pennies, nickels, and dimes to ride for a little while. It was really a treat at that time to go riding in a T-model Ford. We didn't try to see how fast it would go. Our pride was taken in how slow we could make the motor turn over and keep the car moving. Two, three, or four miles per hour was considered real good, and we would ride up Prince Avenue as slow as it was possible to go; if another crowd went a little slower than we did, we would take the whole motor apart trying for a slower gait.

One time I was tuning our old Ford, and I told a cousin of mine, Richard Collins, to grab the third spark plug to see if it was firing. He was seated on the front fender when he grabbed that plug, and the ensuing shock almost disjointed him. He didn't say a word. He just got up off the ground and went home, and I didn't see him for two days. I almost died laughing.

One tragedy came our way during the early 1920s. Dad and Mom were in the country around Washington, Georgia, in the search for antiques, and Dad found a particularly nice piece of wood. I don't recall whether it was cherry or walnut, but it was rather long and he stuck it in the back seat with the end out on the right side. It stuck out about thirty feet, and Mom remarked that it was dangerous, but Dad said, "Naw, it won't hurt a thing." When they got into the Athens city limits, a woman was walking on what is now Oak Street, and Dad didn't see her. That board caught her in the back of the head and just pulverized the skull. She didn't die, but it was nip and tuck for a while. If a lesser doctor than John Hunnicutt had been on the job, she would have died. That man did a miraculous job in saving that woman's life. Dad never hauled a piece of lumber that way again. It scared him nearly to death to think that he had almost killed someone. That night, while we were waiting to hear whether the woman was going to be all right, no one was allowed to speak to Dad. Aunts, uncles, and cousins gathered together, and we all spoke in hushed tones until finally the phone rang and we were told that she would live. Then all the aunts kissed Dad, and all the uncles and cousins shook his hand and told him how glad they were for him, and we kids all sighed a sigh of relief that our dad wasn't a murderer. Dad had to pay all her medical bills, of course, and we were glad that he was able to.

Once, Dad found a fine piece of furniture that he didn't have the money to buy at the time so he came back home and sold it to one of Athens's most distinguished antiquers, Mr. Albert Sams. The man who owned the desk or whatever had told Dad that he didn't like checks, and when Mr. Sams gave Dad a check, he forgot to go by the bank and cash it. When he got to the man's house to buy the furniture, he told the man, "We don't use anything but cash. We don't believe in anything but cash." He ran his hand in his pocket and when he touched the check he remembered not going by the bank. He looked around at my late Uncle Ernest Poss, licked his lips, pulled out the check, and said, "Now this check is just like gold. There is no cash in the world better than it is." He finally convinced the man to take the check and, just as he had said, it was as good as gold. The incident proves that the only thing on his mind was the furniture. Money was nothing except a means of securing the woodwork he wanted.

Another time, he went to a farmer's house and the farmer told him he had a piece of furniture in his barn but if they went down there they were not to smoke as he had hay in the barn and it was terribly dry at that time. Dad said, "I haven't smoked in a long time. I won't smoke down there." When they entered the barn and he saw the furniture, though, he got so excited he pulled out a cigarette, lit it, and threw the match in the hay on the floor of the barn. That farmer nearly had a heart attack, but the fire was quickly put out, and Dad convinced him it was an accident and bought the furniture.

Dad had an inherent talent for the antiques business and taught many people the art of finding, buying, and knowing the finer points of the trade. Mr. Jake Bernstein was one of his pupils and an able one as he was already in the furniture business. Mr. Bernstein disliked driving his own car so he would get one of his employees to drive for him when he and Dad went on a search for antiques. His cars were always fine, large cars so they could cover a lot more ground than a Ford. One time, we went into the mountains around Tallulah Falls to see some furniture Dad had located, and Mr. Ralph Aaron was driving Mr. Bernstein's car. I was riding up front with Mr. Aaron, and Dad and Mr. Bernstein were in the rear. This was in 1928 when I was thirteen years old. I had been smoking about a year, and I was having a nicotine fit because everyone in the car was smoking except me. I finally could stand it no longer so I asked Mr. Aaron to give me a cigarette. He did and Dad asked, "How long you been smoking, boy?" I said about a year, and that is the only time he ever mentioned smoking to me. He was a rare person in that he would smoke for a year and then quit for a year. I never knew him to smoke for two years in a row.

Dad was born in the foothills of the Appalachians and spent his early childhood around Gainesville and Lula, Georgia. Grandpa Thomas came to Athens in the early 1900s and built the houses now standing on the northwest and northeast corners of Nacoochee and Boulevard. My dad and his brothers John and Tillman hauled the lumber from Lula to Athens by ox cart to build these two houses. In 1906, my dad started building the house at 835 Boulevard. He married my mom in 1907, and they moved into their honeymoon house. While living there, they became the parents of two girls, Dorothy and Mildred, then moved to the top of Boulevard Hill in what is now known as the Smith house, where Sarah and I were born.

My grandfather Epps gave my mother a farm of twenty-five acres on the old Epps Bridge Road, and we lived there for about two years, then moved January 1, 1919, to 245 Nacoochee Avenue, where my mother still lives. My dad had been riding a bicycle to work from the farm, and he had two bicycles so when we moved to Nacoochee, he used to rent them out on Sundays to people who worked in the old cotton mill at the intersection of Hiawassee Avenue and the Seabord Railroad.

There were six of us until 1921, when Eugenia was born, and for six years she was the baby. Then Jo Anne came along, and she stayed the baby of the family. Mom and Dad had six children, two born in each house, and two born in March, two in July, and two in September. Coincidentally one from each house and one from each month was dead with cancer by the year 1953. Then after Dad's death our oldest sister was killed in an automobile wreck. That leaves of our family Mom, Jo Anne, and me. The three of us are avowed fanatics about antiques, and we conduct auctions and attend auctions whenever and wherever possible. We are not dealers, not collectors, but just accumulators of antiques. Dad rubbed off on us in spite of ourselves.

I despised the business when I was very young because Dad made me help him work on the furniture and I hated that work with a passion. I wanted to play with the other kids in the neighborhood, and when I could slip away I would stay gone until almost dark so I wouldn't have to help. If hindsight wasn't better than foresight, we would all be rich, and so it is with me. I look back and see that I should have learned everything I had the opportunity to learn from Dad. His knowledge of the periods and patterns of furniture was phenomenal.

After a while at the Nacoochee house, Dad decided he needed a shop so he built one in the backyard. Not long after, he bought a pool table and installed it there. My uncles and friends used to gather there at night to play pool and generally have a good time. That was my first experience at playing pool. I used to carry an apple box around the table with me and climb up on it to shoot. That training has come in very handy. I have played pool with men who were called "sharks," and not one of them has ever made a dime off me. I get ashamed of taking their money when they are supposed to be the pros and me an amateur.

Mom got tired of the pool games after a while, and one night she went on the back porch. She had Dad's pistol, and she fired two shots through the roof. Men came out the windows, doors, and every way imaginable. Mom laughed and laughed about that. Dad called the men and said, "It's only Ethel, boys. Come on back," but to a man they replied, "That's okay, Shorty. We'll see you later."

Well, Mama broke up the nightly pool games, and then when Dad started working with antiques the pool table had to go. My dad finally came into his own when he entered the antiques business. It was as if he had been hunting it all his life. As the young say today, "it was his thing," and he was happiest when hunting antiques and working on them, either repairing or reproducing them. He always said that if a reproduction was 75 percent old wood it was truly an antique, and sometimes he would hunt for weeks to find the proper old piece of furniture to have the right wood to finish a fine reproduction.

Mr. Henry Green, who is a very prominent buyer of rare antiques for museums, bought many fine pieces of furniture from Dad. Very often, Dad would find the particular piece he wanted and then take Mr. Green to see the owner and buy it directly from him or her. For this, of course, Mr. Green always paid Dad a generous commission.

While Dad was the artist, Mom was the business manager, and she had rough sledding sometimes. It was she who had to face the bill collectors and put them off for another week and take a few cents and stretch them to buy enough groceries for a meal for eight people. Somehow she always managed to keep us fed.

I had a very large flock of chickens at this time, and they all came from two small bantam hens and a rooster. A friend of mine in the neighborhood had a few white leghorns. All our chickens ran loose. Well, my two little hens just couldn't resist the beauty of that fine white leghorn rooster; they were prolific setters, and every few weeks one or the other would show up with ten to fourteen chicks. Eventually this flock grew to about a hundred. They all would lay under the houses in the neighborhood, and most any given day I could go out with a basket and come back with several dozen eggs. These eggs and young fryers really helped out, and they helped the neighbors, too, because the chickens roamed all over and were open game for anyone. I never counted them or cared if a few were eaten by others because we had so many.

Mom always had a good garden, and for several years we had a cow and most times one or two pigs so I don't guess we fared so badly. Clothes were the things we missed most. We were covered but not in the latest styles. All our everyday toys were homemade, and at Christmas time I nearly always got a pair of skates and my sisters would get dolls. One bleak Christmas, I wanted an electric train so badly. I hoped and prayed that I would somehow get one, but there wasn't enough money for the necessities, let alone an electric train. Christmas morning I got up and my present was one of the small plate-sized tin trays with a wind-up train going round and round. There were good Christmasses too, like the one when I got a very large tricycle that my high-falutin aunts said I should call a Velocipede. That same Christmas, Dot, my oldest sister, got a new bicycle, and Mildred and Sarah got dolls. We really felt rich that time. Alas, I finally grew up to the ripe old age of eleven and from then on I got only clothes for Christmas—a suit and a pair of shoes that cost my parents about fifteen dollars total—no more toys for me after that. At the time, I didn't realize how hard a struggle it was for Mom and Dad even to pay that small amount. Dad never in his life knew the value of a dollar for anything except shop work on antiques and for buying more antiques.

Dad wasn't a regular churchgoer, but he had a deep belief in God and his words in the Bible. I have never met a confirmed wood lover who didn't believe. They see the beauty of God in the beautiful delicate grain of the woods they work with, and they inherently know that a force far greater than man created this magnificence.

Sometimes when Dad would make me go to the country with him, I hated it because I had things I wanted to do, but I had to go anyway. I always swore that I wouldn't ever do this when I got grown. One day, many, many years later, I went west of Athens and bought the entire contents of a man's house. I was coming into town with my truck loaded down, and all of a sudden the memory hit me and I laughed and laughed about it. There I was, doing exactly what my dad had done, and was very proud of the privilege.

I wish I had paid more attention to Dad. I would have been a better man for it. He tried to teach me all the fundamentals of antiques, and quite a lot of it stuck, but a lot got away from me. Some people knew more about antiques than Dad did, but they were few and far between. People beat a path to his door to ask his advice on different styles and makes of furniture, and he never refused to help them if he could.

  He wasn't an angel, and he wasn't a devil. He was just my dad.

Checklist of the Exhibition

All works by Henry Eugene Thomas (1883-1965), unless otherwise noted.

Breakfront, 1950
Commissioned and codesigned by
Henry D. Green (1909-2003)
Mahogany, poplar, and yellow pine
94 x 20 ¼ x 77 ½ inches
Private collection

Cabinet, n.d.
Walnut
29 ¾ x 23 ½ x 16 ¼ inches
Collection of Mr. and Mrs. Glenn
and Linda Paul

Chest of drawers, n.d.
Walnut and yellow pine
41 ¾ x 43 ⅜ x 22 ¾ inches
Collection of Mr. and Mrs. Arthur
Thomas Kittle

Clock, ca. 1940
Combination of woods including
maple, walnut, and mahogany veneer
29 ⅝ x 16 ½ x 4 ¼ inches
Collection of Mr. and Mrs. Glenn
and Linda Paul

Mantel clock, n.d.
Walnut, book matched mahogany
veneer, probably maple, and ivory
or bone escutcheon
31 ⅝ x 17 ½ x 4 ½ inches
Collection of Mr. James Thomas
Puckett, grandson of Henry
Eugene Thomas

Gothic Revival mantel clock, n.d.
Unidentified mixed woods
19 x 10 ⅝ x 4 inches
Collection of Mr. James Thomas
Puckett, grandson of Henry
Eugene Thomas

Coffee table, ca. 1957
Codesigned by Marion West Marshall
(1928-1964)
Walnut, white pine, and yellow pine
18 ⅞ x 17 ⅞ x 51 inches
Collection of George O. Marshall Jr.
and Charlotte Thomas Marshall

Desk, ca. 1936
Walnut, poplar, yellow pine,
and possibly white pine
56 ½ x 36 1/16 x 20 ¾ inches
Private collection

Desk, ca. 1951
Cherry, walnut veneer; poplar,
probably white pine, ring porous
wood (probably chestnut), and
mixed woods
53 ⅛ x 34 ¾ x 20 ⅝ inches
Collection of Carol Bland Dolson

Desk, ca. 1947-53
Walnut
38 ⅛ x 39 x 19 inches
Collection of the Morris W. H.
Collins Jr. family

Desk, ca. 1930
Cherry and yellow pine
41 ½ x 38 3/16 x 21 ¼ inches
Collection of Laura Kittle Hunter

Mirror, n.d.
Mahogany and/or walnut
with mahogany veneer and
an unidentified soft wood
34 ¼ x 20 ½ x 4 ¼ inches
Collection of Hazel H. Thomas

Sideboard, ca. 1940
Mahogany and various soft woods
40 ⅛ x 73 x 26 ⅜ inches
Collection of Adelaide and
Graham Ponder

Unidentified maker
Table, ca. 1800-30
Walnut, maple, poplar, southern yellow
pine, and crotch mahogany veneer
28 ⅛ x 24 ½ x 18 ⅛ inches
Collection of Mrs. Henry D. Green

Pair of end tables, n.d.
Walnut
28 ¼ x 19 ⅛ x 16 ½ inches, each
Collection of Betty Gorham

Table, n.d.
Walnut
27 ⅜ x 17 13/16 x 16 7/16 inches
Collection of Mr. and Mrs. Glenn
and Linda Paul

Nesting tables, ca. 1940
Walnut
29 x 20 x 16 inches
Collection of John and
Patricia Whitehead

CHECKLIST

Table, n.d.
Probably walnut and unidentified hardwood
30 x 23 (diameter) inches
Collection of Mr. James Thomas Puckett, grandson of Henry Eugene Thomas

Table, n.d.
Probably walnut and unidentified hardwoods
29 x 23 (diameter) inches
Collection of Robbie Thomas

Selected ephemera:

Ethel Epps and Eugene Thomas wedding portrait, 1907
Photograph
5 ½ x 3 ⅞ inches
Collection of Barbara Lumpkin

Arthur V. Clifton (1879–1956, active Athens, Georgia, ca. 1888–1913, then active Atlanta, Georgia)
Portrait of Henry Eugene Thomas, ca. 1910
Photograph mounted on board
Board: 10 x 6 inches; photograph: 5 ⅝ x 3 ⅞ inches
Collection of Frank and Martha Puckett Roberts

Gene and Ethel Thomas, ca. 1920
Photograph
2 ⅞ x 4 ½ inches
Collection of Jill Kittle Thistle

The James R. White Jr. House, 1924
Photograph by Robert Flowers (active Atlanta, Georgia)
2 ⅝ x 4 ⅝ inches
Private collection

Thomas family, ca. 1935 (l–r standing: Gene, Ethel, Dot, Mildred, Sarah, Jack; l–r seated: Jo Anne, Eugenia)
Photograph
3 ½ x 4 ⅞ inches
Collection of Hazel H. Thomas

Business card, n.d.
2 ⅜ x 3 ⅞ inches
Collection of Hazel H. Thomas

Jack Thomas and Gene Thomas, ca. 1940
Photograph
5 1/16 x 3 ½ inches
Collection of Hazel H. Thomas

Gene Thomas, ca. 1940
Photograph
5 1/16 x 3 9/16 inches
Collection of Hazel H. Thomas

Vintage postcard of the home of Dr. Harry E. Talmadge, Athens, Georgia, n.d. Published by the Asheville Post Card Company (Asheville, North Carolina)
3 ½ x 5 ½ inches
Private collection

Richard, Laura, and Jo Anne Kittle, ca. 1948
Photograph
Collection of Jill Kittle Thistle

Gene Thomas with his granddaughter Laura Kittle, ca. 1948
Photograph
3 9/16 x 2 ½ inches
Collection of Laura Kittle Hunter

Laura Kittle with an antique chair outside of Gene Thomas's shop, ca. 1948
Photograph
3 9/16 x 2 ½ inches
Collection of Laura Kittle Hunter

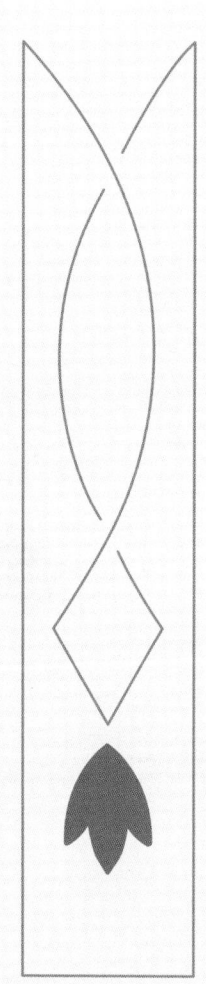